COUNTING THE COST

A Family in the Miners' Strike

Jackie Keating

Wharncliffe Publishing Limited

To Don with love.

First published in 1991 by
Wharncliffe Publishing Limited
47 Church Street, Barnsley,
South Yorkshire S70 2AS.

ISBN: 1 871647 10 X

*For up-to-date information on other titles produced under
the Wharncliffe Publishing imprint, please telephone or
write to:*

> **Wharncliffe Publishing Limited**
> FREEPOST, 47 Church Street
> Barnsley, South Yorkshire S70 2BR
> Telephone (24 hours): 0226-734555

Printed by Yorkshire Web
(A Division of the Barnsley Chronicle Limited)

A CIP catalogue record of this book is available from
the British Library.

Front cover Photograph: Courtesy of John Marshall
Graphics: Paul Morton
Design: Roni Wilkinson

ACKNOWLEDGEMENTS

I would like to thank the following people for their consideration, generosity, but most of all, for caring. They will be forever in my thoughts.

Dee Mitchell, Sue Gardener, Frank Shepherd, Cyril Webb, Brampton firemen and the F.B.U. visitors — especially my unnamed friend. DJ Carl of the Tree Top Road Show. Steve and Betty Wileman (ex Junction Inn). All my family, friends (old and new) and neighbours.

My grateful thanks to Gareth Pearce, Mike McLaughlin and Mike Mansfield whose dedication helped Don and other miners reach a 'just' verdict.

A special thankyou also to Sheila Morton, Richard Wells, Brian Lewis and everyone at the Yorkshire Art Circus, and finally John Threlkeld and everyone at Wharncliffe Publishing, but for them this book would never have reached publication.

CONTENTS

FOREWORD

The Miners' Strike of 1984/85 split communities, families and lips. It brought the author and myself together.

The suspicion and hostility of striking mineworkers towards the media made coverage of the dispute by journalists, particularly a television journalist, difficult and at times dangerous.

Jackie Keating (after our first 'chance' meeting in her local grocery shop) and her neighbours, brought a quiet reasoning of the issues behind their husbands' industrial action, which rang louder in the ears of a bewildered nation than a thousand braying pickets could ever do.

The Miners' Strike was about more than headline-grabbing stories of mass pickets at Orgreave, of violence outside colliery gates, of deaths and of scabs. It wasn't about the miners' leader Arthur Scargill locked in conflict with Margaret Thatcher and her government.

It was about concerned and frightened pit communities, like the one surrounding Cortonwood Colliery, of which the author is a part; concerned about their men's jobs, frightened for a future in which there was to be no place for the only livelihoods they had ever known — digging coal.

Cortonwood Colliery, the catalyst of the Miners' Strike, does not exist today. The redundant, rusting winding gear and the surface buildings were razed by the then National Coal Board within weeks of the dispute ending, as if physical obliteration could erase the pain of twelve months on strike. It has not. Pits continue to close; miners are taking their redundancy cheques with barely a whimper of protest and with little idea of what to do in the future.

When the miners of Cortonwood decided to fight the closure of their colliery, in the early spring of 1984, fifty-eight pits produced coal in Yorkshire; 55,000 miners worked in them. Six years later, the number of pits had shrunk to thirty-one. Thirty-four thousand colliers' jobs had been lost.

A period of rehabilitation is now under way. Environmentally, a mixture of national government and European Community money is providing a salve to heal the physical scars of a county with a long history of digging for coal. The economic and social readjustments which are necessary will take longer, and no doubt come with greater difficulty. Mining communities in Yorkshire have still much to experience . . . after the Miners' Strike.

Richard Wells

CHAPTER ONE

Dumbfounded
'They're shutting Cortonwood down'

I live in a mining village called Brampton, in the heart of the Yorkshire coal field. It is a quiet, relaxed environment of no specific significance to anyone, apart from the local inhabitants. The village's way of life hadn't changed in decades. The National Coal Board had been and still was the main employer in our region. My husband, Don, started work in Cortonwood Colliery in 1977.

The first of March 1984 was just a normal day for me and my family. My children Nikki (11) and Darren (9) had been to school as usual, then we had a quiet evening at home in front of a roaring fire. It was early March and the weather was still quite cold. Looking back, there wasn't a thing to point out that in a few hours our quiet, peaceful life would be literally ripped apart. The children and I waved Don off to his night shift, each in turn wishing him goodnight with a kiss and my usual 'Take care, love'. After the usual round of tucking the children in, locking up, damping down the fire for the night, I went to bed for the last peaceful night I was to have for a very long time.

The first inkling I had of something out of the ordinary was Don shaking me awake. He would never deliberately wake me up, and usually was extremely quiet, not to do so. 'Get up Jackie, I want to talk to you.' I dragged myself downstairs where Don was poking the fire to bring it back to life. Sitting down, he passed a cup of tea which he had waiting for me. 'They're shutting Cortonwood down on April 6th.'

I just couldn't believe it. How? When? Why? So many questions flooded into my head. In shock, Don and I carried on talking for a couple of more hours until the children got up to go to school. All our questions still left unanswered, Don finally went to bed to try to sleep, leaving me to breakfast the children and see them off to school. All this time I kept thinking and trying to make sense of it all.

For the last year Don and three other men had been working on a pipe-line which ran from the shaft top, right the full length to the pit bottom — approximately 2000 metres. This was very costly, not only in material but also the men's wages, which included a lot of overtime payments. Also there had been huge expenditure on new baths, including tiles and showers, with everything refitted. If they were going to shut the pit down, who had given the go-ahead to spend all this unnecessary money, only on completion to announce the closure, so that bulldozers could knock the lot down — sheer lunacy! It made as much sense as a family spending vast amounts of money on a house to fit it out with every modern convenience, only to order it demolished on completion. No one in their right mind would do that, would they? It wasn't unusual for the NCB to waste vast amounts of money. The management would hire a large piece of equipment, for example a coal-cutting machine, and when it had finished whatever job it had been hired to do, instead of it being taken back off the face and either sent back to where it was hired from or moved to another working area, it would be abandoned, which would usually result in it being crushed by the weight from the roof of the coal face and left to rust. The NCB would still be paying the hire fees for many more years.

The news spread like wildfire. A lot of my friends and neighbours gathered in groups in Dearne Road, Brampton, after taking their little ones to school. Everyone was dumbfounded. The NCB had not said anything about the men's jobs or possible transfers. No one knew anything. Each of the girls were coming up with her own interpretation. When the men came home from the day shift, they still weren't any wiser. None of the Union men knew anything either. In fact the story goes that the local delegate was stopped whilst driving in to work and the news was then broken to him.

I don't remember much more about that day, or most of the following days. They passed almost in a haze — the worry was terrible.

I remember ringing Don's Mum and Stepfather Albert, to give them the news. 'Mum, I'm ringing to tell you Cortonwood is closing down. I wanted to tell you myself rather than you finding out on television.' On reflection I have a quiet grimace to myself, because not only did she hear about it — everyone carried on hearing about it for one whole year. And there was the terrible effect it had on our own family, because Don's family live in Nottingham and one of our brothers-in-law also works for the NCB, but in the Nottinghamshire coalfield.

I must say at this point that, because of the pain and hardship which was suffered, not only by myself but by my family, friends and neighbours, I can never forgive the faceless people who deliberately planned with terrible callousness and vindictiveness to inflict as much suffering on as many mining communities as possible, with no exceptions. I'm not going to go into Mr Scargill's or Mr MacGregor's or the Government's role in the strike, only when I was personally affected by them.

Don is not only a miner, he is also a retained fireman, so unlike most families we did have some income each month. I also worked in a cafe, earning £17.50 a week. This meant the world to us, because we were still supporting our family ourselves. Since our marriage in 1972 we have always supported ourselves, including paying for our wedding. Apart from a few wedding presents, everything we have has been physically earned, mainly by Don. To us, this is the right way to go on in life. If you're old enough to marry, you're old enough to go it alone. The only exception was the children having to have free school meals. This was a fact we had to accept because we couldn't have found the extra money for them.

Life for the first couple of weeks I remember being filled with worry, coping financially, keeping our behaviour as normal as possible for our children. Each news bulletin was watched anxiously for any change. My friends and neighbours would stop and discuss it for hours — how to cope, how to make the money stretch a bit further.

Easter was the first time I remember our family being in a small crisis. The Parish Council had provided Easter eggs for all the children in Brampton, working people's children as well as those of dole families. It was an ordinary sort of day. I was busy washing, as usual on my day off work, when Sue, a neighbour, called in to see if I was going up to the local Village Hall to collect an egg each for my children. Since the notice had gone up in the village about the eggs, Don had been really quiet about the subject, although I knew it was on his mind. After Sue's enquiry I said to her, 'I will catch you up, you go on ahead.' After she had left Don said, 'We don't beg for anything, Jackie.' I replied quietly that I couldn't bear to see the children without an egg on Easter morning. As I walked out of the door to catch up with Sue, I knew I had hurt my husband terribly. He is a very proud man and if he couldn't provide for us, then we would go without. I will never forget my husband's face at that moment; he was so choked with hurt that I could betray him like that. It wasn't easy entering the hall and asking for the eggs, but my love for my children comes foremost and if my pride had to suffer, then so be it. I must say that my fear that the children wouldn't receive an egg on Easter morning wasn't justified, as three others were bought for them by family not involved in the strike, even though we couldn't afford to buy our nephews and nieces any that year.

It was obvious to everyone directly involved in the strike that it was going to be a prolonged dispute. Almost simultaneously, across the mining communities the women formed themselves into groups to offer help and support in any and all ways possible.

I think it was sometime in April when Brampton's Soup Kitchen started, along with the food parcels. I became involved myself in the Action Group because our husbands needed support apart from just physically feeding them, important though that was; even more so for the single miners because they didn't receive a single penny from anywhere. I approached a couple of friends, Jenny Evans and Helen Hargreaves, who agreed it was equally important to show our support through rallies and the like. We began by having posters made to get like-minded women to join us in our enterprise. Then we approached the NUM delegates to ask where we could be of some assistance. After helping to acquire a few things for the food kitchens, like crockery and cutlery, not a lot was really needed as they had it quite well planned by this time.

The next thing we did was to contact the other groups in Barnsley and Rotherham. We contacted both areas to learn from their experience, as they had been going longer. During this time a friend took me to one side and said, 'Your heart's in the right place, but you're going to have to be tough to see this group through.' I didn't understand at the time, but I found out the veiled meaning sooner rather than later.

The local branch president of the NUM asked Jenny, Helen and me to help with a television reporter. A meeting was set up in Cortonwood's strike centre to discuss a programme he had in mind. He wanted to live with a family in Brampton to find out what made us all tick, why we were on strike and how we were managing. Full of enthusiasm, I went home to ask if he could stay with us. Wow! Did the balloon go up! My husband, who is usually quite a placid man, flew into a terrible rage. 'How could you ask, Jackie? They are all nothing but a bunch of wallies. Not one of them cares a damn about the truth!' I had known Don had a dislike of media people, but to class them all the same was as damning as classing all miners as thugs. It didn't matter how quietly or sensibly I tried to talk to him, he was adamant. 'No bloody press men or telly men are going to enter my house.'

I'm not a person to row much, I would prefer to prove my own point. It may take a long time, but like the proverbial tortoise, I try to get there in the end. (The trouble that got me into!) I set out to find a family for him to live with, but was very upset because I had to ask someone else to do what I couldn't. I tried a couple of people but finally asked the family of one of the founding leaders of the food kitchens. So with the usual warm-hearted Yorkshire generosity, he was welcomed to stay, but after a couple of days I had to rehouse him because the family didn't have a telephone and it was vital for him to keep in touch with his base in London. Unfortunately, he was recalled shortly afterwards because someone else was doing a similar thing in Wales.

The second time I came in contact with the press was a meeting again in the strike centre (Don had agreed to me meeting the press people, providing it wasn't at home). A man called Kim from the *Sunday Times* met us there. I found him to be a nice person, but I doubted at the time if he had truly understood what I was trying to say. How I wished I was articulate, so many things to say, but how to make people understand that all we wanted was the right to work. Incidentally, I saw him being interviewed by television reporters, standing on a picket line, defending the jobs of the printers in the Wapping dispute. Ironic, really.

CHAPTER TWO

Survival
'Selling the furniture'

As well as the worry of our own family, my parents and youngest brother, Alan, were also involved in the miners' strike. We worried about them constantly. My mum received £6.50 a week. £1.30 of this was supposed to be taken out and saved towards the water rates. The council house rent was also paid. I hasten to say the water rates weren't paid because, by no stretch of the imagination could three adults and a dog be fed on £5.20 a week. We tried to help each week by buying bread and a few items, but being hard-up ourselves, with children to feed, it really wasn't a great deal. Also, if the DHSS had found out they would have deducted the cost from the small amount they allowed.

How did the DHSS arrive at the princely sum, deemed to be enough to live on? Well, no miner was allowed any money whatsoever. The wife was allowed £21.50. £15.00 was deducted because the Government decreed that the Union would pay £15.00 each week out of Union funds (money we didn't receive). I don't know if anyone can imagine living for one month on £6.50 a week, let alone for a year. As it happens the family survived for seven months on this money. For it was my brother's sad misfortune which made them a bit better off financially by his getting sickness benefit. An eye disease he had as a child flared up again. His eyesight carried on deteriorating to such an extent that the eye specialist couldn't help any more and told him to be prepared to wake up one morning totally blind.

The only good news — if you could call it that — was being able to claim benefit. What devastating news, the realisation that at any moment you would never see daylight again.

He received approximately £24.00 a week. He gave £15 to mum to try to help pay off some of the electricity bill so they wouldn't be cut off. The rest he needed to pay for his prescriptions and travelling expenses to Sheffield to see the specialist.

The day that is engraved on my mind is the day a friend of my parents stopped me while I was walking from Wombwell back to my own village of Brampton. 'Do you know that your Mum and Dad are advertising quite a few things to sell out of the house?' I knew things had been hard for them, especially when the bills came in, but to come to this! I was so heartbroken, for I knew how many hours Dad had to go down into the mine for each piece of furniture. I remember walking home, tears streaming down my face, thinking — we just couldn't help any more. Don was working in the garden when I arrived home, and demanded to know what was wrong. After I had calmed down a little, I explained what had happened. Who to ask? That was the question, for most of the family was also involved in the strike; I have three brothers in all. The eldest, Malcolm, stopped visiting my parents at the onset of the strike. Garry, who works for British Telecom, is two years younger than I am, he was also helping Mum and Dad. Alan, the youngest, is the one who is a miner. After a lot of discussion the decision had to be between asking Garry for even more help, or approaching Mum's only surviving relative, a sister who lives down South. Should I 'phone her? What about Malcolm? Not a chance — if he could desert them at a time of crisis, then he really wasn't worth bothering with. In the end I went to see my brother Garry and his wife Ann. I remember breaking down, asking him for some more money for my parents, because in the back of my mind I knew I would be hurting Dad. Dad, like Don, is extremely proud and would literally starve rather than ask any man, even his own son, to help him. Garry was appalled that he would sell every stick of furniture rather than ask for help. Indeed, he was very hurt, and went to help very quickly.

My own personal pride by this time was in shreds around my feet. I seem to make a habit of hurting the men in my family in my efforts to help them.

Roy Hart, the president of the local branch of the NUM, approached me to ask if we — the family — would go to a Labour Party meeting in Leeds. A host of stars would be appearing, as well as Neil and Glenys Kinnock. It was quite a memorable day, there was entertainment, and during the interval the men went into conference with Neil Kinnock, and I found myself sitting next to his wife, talking about ordinary things. She was extremely anxious not to miss their scheduled train home to London, because she had so much housework to catch up on. To me she seemed a very nice person coping beautifully with combining a career, motherhood, housewifely duties, and still managing to lend her full support to her husband, like most wives.

Unfortunately, the trip to Leeds was to be the starting point of the separation with the Action Group that was to come. Looking back, I see that my lack of experience contributed to the problems: having never belonged to any kind of committee, I didn't have a clue about rules and regulations. Some of the ladies took exception to my family and I being invited to meet Neil Kinnock, so they had a meeting during my absence. At the following meeting, a few days later, a big disagreement blew up about an evening I had begun to organise, and the costing of the Pea and Pie Supper for the evening. A friend of mine knew someone in the catering business and had been very helpful in enabling me to provide a portion per person for 12½p. Their costing for buying the materials and home-baking, including fuel, was a lot more. To make a profit, to give us money for rallies, I suggested a charge of 25p per portion. A reasonable cost, because an acquaintance, a local disc-jockey, kindly provided free music. Plus I had visited the local shops to ask for donations of sweets to give to the children. Not only was I outvoted, but they had already purchased the materials during my absence. The charge was to be 50p per portion. I was sick with hurt. How could they, knowing how hard it was for the families just to exist, let alone enjoy the luxury of an evening out. Most of the families had two, three or even four children. How on earth would they be able to come? My aim had been to give the people of Brampton a lovely evening out, to have a break from the rigours of the strike, and in doing so to bring in some funds. After a terrible scene — I was adamant they wouldn't make use of my hard work — I was told to go ahead. I could do it alone.

There I was, left to somehow provide 200 portions of pies and peas. Luckily everything else was already organised. It was pretty difficult to find anywhere for it to be held which would cost nothing. The licensing hours meant we needed to find a pub with facilities for children. The perfect venue was the Junction Inn, which had a large garden containing climbing frames and quite a number of swings. Steve and Betty, who ran it, were smashing. They gave me a lot of moral support which I badly needed by this time. My husband, brother and close friends all rallied around me. It was their loyal support which helped me through the days that followed — I worried so much, I hardly slept.

The problems seemed insurmountable: Money to purchase the pies and peas? How and where to actually warm or cook them? Transportation and, last but not least, how to keep them all warm?

The money — the first problem — was solved by borrowing Don's fire station money. He was paid monthly, so we used to draw out a small amount each week to help feed the family.

The rest was left in to pay at least part of the bills, so we wouldn't be cut off. I took the money, knowing full well that if the people of Brampton decided to boycott the evening my family would be eating pie and peas for ever and a day. I wondered how many pies and peas per therm of electricity. I was frightened about taking the little money we had to feed our own children to put on a fund-raising project which could easily backfire on me. My friend's warning came right back. I don't regret standing up to the women who had been at that fateful meeting. Then, and now, I believe people matter, money comes a poor second.

Soaking and cooking the peas was achieved by dishing out two pounds of dried peas to a number of my neighbours who duly dealt with them. The same people also warmed the pies. To keep everything warm, I borrowed three cool boxes for the pies and lined them with tin foil. The logic in that was to keep the heat in, rather than out. Two large plastic bins used in the catering business were commissioned for the peas, after they had been sterilised of course! Hygiene was uppermost in my mind, I didn't want anyone to get ill enjoying themselves. The responsibility was all on my shoulders for this and it grew steadily heavier as the days passed — I worried so much I felt really ill. Needless worry, because the evening was a wonderful success. The weather was glorious and many, many people turned up. All the pies and peas were sold; I had underestimated if anything.

It's the children that really stick out in my mind. The air was full with their laughter. Carl, the DJ, provided prizes for games and threw them around quite generously. We had so many sweets donated that the children had more than they could hold, let alone eat. They — the happy children— mattered more to me than the £79 profit we made, over and above the money I gave back to my husband and after paying for sauces, spoons and dishes. The most embarrassing thing about the evening, and most unexpected, was when Dougie Robertson, a NUM official, dragged me out into the middle of the garden and thanked me profusely, then everyone applauded. I wanted the ground to open up and swallow me whole. I was grimy from selling the wretched pie and peas all evening, and my feet were aching. Looking a complete mess, I bolted out of that garden like a frightened rabbit, which caused more of a laugh than if I had stayed where I was. I must have been at the back of the queue when sophistication and decorum were passed out!

The following day I took the money to the newly-elected treasurer and then resigned; their ways and mine were completely different. I was very disillusioned about the whole thing. After a great deal of thought since then, I now know that I was technically wrong. I should have accepted the decision which had gone against me. However, the other women were not without fault. The correct way to resolve such a problem was to have a quorum of members present to vote. If the problem was still left unresolved, it should then have gone to all group members. Nevertheless I am pleased with the direction I took and have no regrets on that particular issue — putting people first. The main lesson I learnt from all of this was that I would make a bad business-woman. The action group carried on regardless, giving the men a great deal of backing, so all was not lost.

CHAPTER THREE

Rallies
'These kids aren't going to get hurt'

Rallies were part of the strike and I found these particularly hard. I went on maybe four or five rallies in all. The first I went to, Mum joined me — something she had never contemplated doing. Mum, like me, felt we should be seen showing our support for our husbands in their struggle. Rallies, we soon realised, were totally out of our league. Listening to the abuse of some of the women to the police made my toes curl, appalled is an understatement. We had both been brought up to be polite, civil, and at all times courteous to all members of the police force. Some of the pit language used against them made me ashamed. I couldn't find it in me to join in the abusive songs being chanted during the march either. I'm not saying the other women didn't have grounds or reason for doing this, only that I didn't like doing it one bit.

During the rally around Barnsley, I found the local people very warm and welcoming. The Sheffield rally I found very uncomfortable — the reception there was cold and, at times, downright hostile.

Mansfield was an education in itself. I felt like an alien from a different planet, and Mum, Dad and Don accompanied me on this one. The abuse was obscene, the women were called anything from prostitute to things much worse, with as many expletives anyone in the world could think about. Old women stood at their gates shaking fists, one in particular stood with her tongue out at any coaches which passed by. Men two-fingered anyone looking out of the coach windows, including small children. The police I can only describe as the lowest of the low. The police are supposed to be well-educated pillars of society. Miners are not by any means angels, but truly the gestures made by the guardians of the law to the coaches were disgusting. Moronic is still not strong enough a word to describe their behaviour on that occasion. I believe it was this attitude which caused the violence that followed later that day at the end of the rally.

Most of the coaches had left and we were still waiting for stragglers, talk about women talking for hours, some men are ten times worse. Everyone was on board when it happened.

To the left of the coach, two young lads of maybe eighteen years of age were being pushed around by three or four police officers. The other two coaches still left suddenly started emptying, their passengers going to the youngsters' rescue. Police suddenly appeared from all directions which suggested that it had already been planned in advance. Men and police were fighting everywhere, women and children started screaming as they battled it out. Many of the miners had truncheons cracked over their heads. The police were like a howling pack of animals, some of the police officers were obviously enjoying themselves immensely. It's that which always comes back to the forefront of my mind when I think about it. Our coach driver slammed the doors shut and wouldn't open them for anyone; realising about the emergency door, he took his chance between the fighting to drive out of the car park at high speed. 'These kids aren't going to get hurt if I can help it,' he said. Congratulations to that man, he kept his head and stopped more problems developing. His care of his passengers was a credit to him.

Returning home to hear about it on television, the story was totally opposite to what we had all witnessed. The trouble had started with drunken miners going berserk and attacking police

22

officers. Shame be always on them — if they can't tell the truth then they shouldn't bother producing a news story at all.

Mum and I went on our fourth rally together, this one being in Wales. On our arrival we walked what seemed like hundreds of miles. The police had routed the rally out into the countryside. It was an extremely hot day and the journey had already been hot and sticky and most of the drinks the girls had taken had already been consumed — no money to buy any more either. This journey had been different because other action groups had been picked up on the way. Already on the coach was Ann Scargill, some students and friends. They were in charge of the coach and groups. On arrival we were told to be back at the coach for 2 o'clock. The walk, as I said, was very long and very hot so we didn't arrive back to the large meeting place until just before 2 o'clock. The 'Speaker' was standing by to go on to the rostrum, when some of the students turned up, very annoyed, to put it mildly. Back at the coach we were told that the driver had to be back for five o'clock and we were irresponsible not being back on time. Four-thirty, nearly home, the coach pulled into a motorway cafe. There, one group disembarked to order some meals, leaving the rest of the ladies on the hot airless bus on the steaming tarmac. Everyone was hungry and dying of thirst by this time. No money to buy anything ourselves. I was so angry I didn't think it possible to feel such rage — you don't do that to people! Those ladies had given their last pennies to show their backing in the strike to their men and Union, only to find the luckier ones had so little regard for the poverty incurred in doing so.

Mum and I never went on another rally. I didn't want to be associated with this kind of attitude. Sadly, yet another avenue had closed to my efforts to show my love and support to the man who means the whole world to me. In retrospect, I was probably wrong to judge that group of women so harshly. Maybe they were preoccupied with their own problems and simply didn't give the other ladies a second thought.

CHAPTER FOUR

The Media
'Did I see you on TV last night?'

I met the media for what I thought was the final time during the last couple of weeks with the Action Group. The first, Triona Holden, was from BBC Radio, based in London. Jenny and I, acting as representatives for Brampton's group, arranged to meet her opposite the cinema in Barnsley's town centre. We were introduced to Triona and one of the members of Barnsley's action group, then driven on to another local town called Hoyland, where we were asked into the house of a lady from Barnsley's group. We met two more women, were given the proverbial cup of tea, then interviewed in turn.

This was the first time I had actually been recorded so I felt self-conscious, and the resulting interview sounded — at least to my ears — strained and full of pauses. I had tried to give a picture of how my parents and people like them were coping. I felt I hadn't succeeded very well.

The second media person was Richard Wells. I met him by accident, or should I say accidentally on purpose, via a local shopkeeper 'friend' of mine.

After completing my household chores I had changed and was on my way up to visit my parents, the rest of my family being at school or on some errand or other. It was a beautiful spring day and I was looking forward to the walk up to Wombwell. I had walked past the local shops when I heard someone shout. Looking round I saw my friend Tilly, the owner of the local off-licence store, gesturing to me to come back.

Knowing Tilly to be very accident prone, I ran back expecting her to have hurt herself in some way. Rushing into the shop I stopped dead in my tracks. Tilly was back behind the counter with a sheepish grin on her face. Standing in front of the counter were three men. One was a tall man about the same height as Don — six feet four — and the other two men were smaller in height, and one was slighter in build than the other, with dark, curly hair. It was obvious that they were a television crew because the tall man had a large camera in his hands.

I knew I had been conned by Tilly, because she knew very well I would think something was wrong and go to her. She introduced me to the man with curly hair, Richard Wells. He introduced me in turn to Ian the camera man and Brian the sound recordist.

Richard asked if I knew of anyone who would be willing to be interviewed about how the strike was going etc. I hadn't changed my views in the least and decided I would try to persuade my friends Jenny, Helen, Sue Garner and Jackie Palfreyman to co-operate. Telling Tilly I would 'see her later', I went out with Richard, giving the other two men my address so they could drive down after stowing their equipment in their blue estate car. In my haste to run to Tilly I hadn't even noticed it sitting on the forecourt. During the walk down Dearne Road I found myself telling him about the different families and how many actually depended on Cortonwood for their living. Glancing up I was very surprised to find he was actually listening — I mean really listening! Instead of the polite surface attention I had felt previously in other media people. For some unknown reason, I also felt quite at ease talking to him, which is unusual for me. Having lived a sheltered life before marriage, and only having had one other boyfriend previous to my husband, I hadn't really ever got over my shyness with the opposite sex. Being at home with my family and not mixing much, even on a social level, hadn't improved the situation. A surprising fact is that no one else has ever really noticed, except Don, because obviously he knows me so well.

It came out during our conversation that Richard and crew were from Look North, BBC's regional news programme. I left them messing about with the equipment in the car whilst I ran up the street to Jenny's house, only to find she was in the bath. I yelled at her to hurry out because it was an emergency — well, if Tilly could do it so could I. I then ran and asked my other three friends if they would come. All, I'm thankful to say, turned up within minutes, including Jenny with her long black hair wrapped in a towel, turban-style, around her head. After making tea, we were then interviewed in the back garden. Everything seemed to go well, not that I knew much about it, and they all left very quickly. Life, I found out, for them, is one mad rush — always in a tearing hurry to meet deadlines — in fact they made me decidedly dizzy at times. If it had been me, I would have asked the world to stop and let me off. It wasn't until after they had gone and I was on my way yet again, that I realised my goose was cooked. How was I going to tell Don that I had invited television people into our home and broken my promise? The fact could hardly be hidden — it was due to be televised that same evening. During my walk up to Mum's I became quite upset; I try always to keep any promises I make. Well, it was too late and the music had to be faced.

Six-thirty came round, following the main evening news, and there I was. I can never tell anyone how embarrassing I found the interview to be, seeing all your own mannerisms you don't realise you have until you actually watch yourself on television. I wished I could be swallowed up by quicksand or something. By the time the interview had finished, Don was rolling almost off his chair, tears streaming down his face. It must have been a funny sight, me with a cushion over my face trying to drown the sound with my hands, saying 'Has it finished yet?' Don, still laughing, said Richard much be quite a guy to have that effect, and could he please come back when football was on. After pulverising him with the cushion in my hands, we eventually watched it again, still no easier I might add. Don laughing at me did heal the slight rift between us caused by my broken promise. After a long discussion he also agreed I could bring home anyone I liked, even the media, so long as he was kept right out of it.

Subsequently Richard got in touch again. This happened at a time when the men of Cortonwood were volunteering to fill coal wagons to keep the steelworks going in Scunthorpe. After interviewing Jenny, Helen, Sue and myself (Jackie Palfreyman, the other girl featured in the first interview, hadn't been too popular with her husband for associating with the television people, so flatly refused to be interviewed for a second time), the crew left post-haste to go down to the mine to see for themselves just what was going on. Our interview was broadcast along with a piece of film showing a coal train leaving with a painted message which said something like 'Sent with love from Cortonwood.' On the interview I had already said that the men were crossing their own picket line to make sure the trains were getting through to Scunthorpe to keep them in work.

During the time we were interviewed, Don spent the entire time upstairs and wouldn't even be introduced. His pig-headedness made me feel angry. Everyone has always been made welcome and our house is known to be an open house to all friends and neighbours. This Don was quite new to me. As they left, Don was on his way downstairs and came face to face with the TV crew. After being briefly introduced Don made some sort of sarcastic comment that the truth never reached the screens. Catching a glimpse of Richard's face I was convinced he would be equally determined to show no bias.

The whole interview went out that evening with the wagon footage. Richard also rang up to ask our opinion, which was nice. How many other people would take their jobs that seriously? I felt really good that night. I had proved that at least one media person could be trusted and I was glad Richard had turned out to be a person with great integrity, and nice with it.

The following day the whole thing rebounded into my face. The same interview had also gone out in the Nottingham area. Some pickets staying with other miners living in that area saw the interview in which I had said the men at Cortonwood are crossing their own picket lines. Nothing more added on to qualify my statement about the coal wagons. They rang up the strike centre to find out just what was going on. They were miles away from home, picketing to try to save jobs to find some of the men had gone back to work! Understandably I took a lot of flak, there were more than enough people — including my husband — only too willing to say I was daft to even trust any media personnel, let alone willingly help them. Most of the people around having seen the undoctored version of the interview realised I couldn't be blamed for the footage being cut in such a bad way.

I was hurt, angry, and felt betrayed. How could Richard Wells use me like that! What a stupid, gullible fool I was. I was equally mad at myself for being such an idiot. Why-oh-why did he have to prove everyone else right, that none of them could be trusted? Seething with rage I got on with the housework. Richard was splattered in every door I slammed and suffocated during the bed making. I was just contemplating into which part of Mr Wells' anatomy I would have liked to ram the toilet brush, when the 'phone rang. It was him, that low-down skunk, Richard Wells. He said he had rung Barnsley's Action Group to try to arrange an interview with Ann Scargill, and had been told that I was out for his blood — quite true — I had spoken about it earlier on the 'phone to the group, asking if anything could be done about it.

Richard wanted to know what was wrong, and hadn't a clue why I was angry. I told him about the cut in the interview down in the Nottingham area. He said they were 'baskets', or something pretty similar, apologising for swearing, and went on to explain that once 'the story' left his own studio there wasn't any guarantee it would go out whole anywhere else because of the timing in their own particular programme. He was as upset about it as I was, either that or he deserved an Oscar for being the world's greatest actor. No, he was genuine about the whole thing, and after hanging up I felt a right heel for doubting him and ashamed that I had been thinking malicious thoughts about him. It didn't alter the fact that I couldn't make things right and put the real interview to the people in the Nottingham area. I was older and wiser from the whole incident.

Richard and crew came a few more times during the year's strike. Don mellowed slightly towards them but it took time and during one visit to the house he was quite nasty and sarcastic to Ian, the camera man, something to do with him running up to the fire station on a fire call. I don't know the whole story but Don's actually said he regretted being so nasty about it.

One thing I remember about their visits was how difficult it was to provide just a basic thing like a cup of tea. The family managed with powdered milk and sweeteners. Neither Don or I liked to offer this kind of tea to other people, so we would scramble around old money boxes, coats and handbags to scrape together enough money for fresh milk and a bag of sugar. Unknown to Don, I would take my sandwich money I needed for work.

I briefly mentioned my work earlier. It was as a waitress in a small cafe in Barnsley town centre three days a week, part-time (4½ hours), where my duties entailed anything from serving meals and snacks, to the drudgery of scouring pots and pans, as well as cleaning the toilet and store room each week. My hours being 10.30 am to 3.00 pm, like the rest of the staff I usually sat down with a cup of tea and a sandwich around 2.00 pm, with the others. So it was pretty obvious why, when I didn't do so. I was so embarrassed when they asked why I wasn't eating, was I feeling ill? Paula the owner was smashing and had a quiet word. She said if ever I was in difficulty I could pay on Friday and not to think any more about it. How I hated doing this — degraded is the word — I've *always* paid my way. They never minded in the least when on occasions this happened, but I did, and a great deal at that.

Tilly and other people would send media people to see us (for some unknown reason the local shops were the starting point for the media for leads to make contact with village people). TV Eye, Channel 4 News, *Rotherham Advertiser*, to name but a few. Don and I never knew the reason why they were sent to our home, we could only surmise that they considered we were able to put the message across, in a way that outside communities could understand. Sometimes there were women present in the crews, but usually they were all male. I found these nerve-racking. I don't know if it was this which made me shake during the interviews or being filmed. Brian, the sound recordist from the Look North team, noticed once, because he was sitting on the floor holding the 'mike' out of shot, when my knees began to knock together. I knew he had noticed, because he looked up at me, but thankfully didn't make any comment.

It was waiting to see how the editing was done that worried the life out of me. I had to trust to the integrity of the unknown media people back at their bases. I didn't want to embarrass my husband, family and friends, as I had previously, with the picket line incident. I never quite got used to strangers stopping me to say 'Did I see you on television last night?' or Don's ceaseless leg-pulling about going out to meet 'Joe Public' whenever I went out of the door. Seriously, I gradually became more and more frustrated with my own inability to put the message across. Maybe if I had had a little more education and experience I wouldn't have found it so hard with all the journalists.

CHAPTER FIVE

Arrested
'Dad wouldn't do anything wrong'

In between those visits by the media, life settled down with Don's and my roles being reversed. I went to work while Don did the household chores. This wasn't difficult for him. His six years in the Grenadier Guards had made him more than capable, and he had always given a hand around the house. The same is true that I shared the gardening and helped to get a ton of coal into the coal shed when the concessionary coal arrived at approximately six-weekly intervals prior to the strike.

Don remained on fire call for almost twenty-four hours a day, because each call-out represented money to keep the family. This however gave vent to guilty feelings about earning money on other people's misfortune. We would willingly starve rather than someone lose their life or property. Luckily most fires are generally non-events, such as false calls or grass fires.

News began to filter back from the flying pickets how badly treated they were, not being allowed near other miners to give them their point of view. Don became more and more restless, he wanted to go picketing, but I was really opposed to him going, and tried my hardest to dissuade him. The problem was he stood out in a crowd, and because he had been televised previously, standing with other miners outside the NUM headquarters in Barnsley, everyone and the cat had seen him, but not his friends standing immediately in front of him. I knew his height, six feet four inches, would automatically draw attention to him.

31

I realised I was wrong to pressurise him; he may be married to me but he was entitled to his own opinions and beliefs. I admired him for wanting to know the truth personally. How many people sit at home, watch television, humming and haa-ing, but never motivate themselves to practise what they preach when giving their own critical views?

Sadly, Don found out there was more than an element of truth in the stories; abuse and beatings were part of a picket's life.

The day I had constantly feared arrived — 18 June 1984. It was a beautiful summer's day. Don had left very early to go to an unknown destination — this was usual, to supposedly outwit the police. I guessed where he was because news bulletins said that there was a mass picket outside a coking plant at Orgreave, near Rotherham. I still hated Don going — but I had accepted that it was what he wanted to do. My tummy would have butterflies and would churn until he arrived home again safe.

That particular day, a working day for me, passed as usual, the housework being completed before I left. As always I went to the shop for a loaf of bread so that Don could have something to eat, should he arrive home before me.

I was walking back down home when I felt a cold shiver run down my spine — I felt that something was wrong. It was one of those moments when you tell yourself not to be so daft, but the feeling couldn't be thrown off. I noticed my cousin's car parked outside his house; this was strange because he should be picketing at the same place as Don. No one answered my knock and I carried on home, still filled with that uneasy, on-edge, and, I suppose, doomed feeling.

I had just finished getting ready for work when the phone rang. It was Don, his voice was grave and quiet, 'I've been arrested Jackie. Listen love, phone the fire station and tell them to take me off call indefinitely.'

'Where are you? Are you all right? What's going to happen?'

I remember yelling down the phone. My heart was beating so loudly I could hardly hear his reply.

'I'm in Sheffield Police Station. Try not to worry. I've got to go now.' The phone clicked and the dialling tone hummed in my ear. I stood there not knowing what to do. Should I go to work? Stay home? I took a deep breath to stop the panicky feeling. Having phoned the fire station, I glanced at my watch and realised I had to make a decision pretty quickly if I was to catch the bus which left in seven minutes' time. Wondering what Don would have done, I could almost hear his reply, with his typical male logic — 'Go to work, we need the money'. With five minutes to spare I ran to catch the bus.

The day at the cafe dragged by, as if in slow motion; every hour seemed like a day and it was a wonder every piece of crockery wasn't broken. Eventually it crawled round to home time. I couldn't wait to get home to be between my own four walls again.

After I got home the phone never stopped ringing, friends of Don asking if I knew about him. I also began to feel they weren't being honest when I asked one or two who had been near to him when he was actually arrested, if he was OK. None of them answered immediately and avoided the question, so I began to feel quite agitated. I rang a neighbour of my parents to ask if Mum would phone me back please. (Mum had been cut off so I couldn't contact her direct.) Normally I would have gone to the house rather than put people out by asking them to run around giving messages, but it was close to the time when the children came home from school and one of us had to be there.

Mum phoned back within minutes, obvious worry in her voice. She had seen the terrible scenes on television as well.

'Is he hurt? Where is he?' I explained what I knew and asked if she would mind coming down to the house to take care of Nikki and Darren. The radio news bulletins had announced that the arrested pickets would appear in Rotherham Magistrates Court later on that day. So I made my mind up to go to the courthouse to see Don and give him moral support. I rang Garry to ask if he would take me, if not I would catch the bus. He said he would be round within a hour; he wanted to shave and change because he had just come in from work. I cooked tea for the children, showered, and changed into a cream suit Don particularly liked me to wear. I wanted and felt I needed to look nice for him especially at a time like this.

Nikki and Darren arrived home from school. It wasn't easy telling them, Darren worships his Dad, and flew into a temper. 'Dad wouldn't do anything wrong! I hate them pigs. I hate them! If they've hurt my dad, I'll kill them,' he said. It took time to calm him down. I also had to remonstrate with him about calling the police 'pigs'. At some time this nightmare would be over and I didn't want them to become used to using abusive language.

Nikki, the quiet one, was crying quietly, sitting on a chair in the corner of the room. 'I know he hasn't done anything wrong. Will they keep him in prison?' I ached to be able to tell them it was all a mistake, a ghastly nightmare, but the truth was, after watching some of the scenes on television, he could be remanded and sent to jail until trial.

Mum arrived, and Garry some minutes later. I hugged and kissed the children; they both clung to me, and knowing they were upset and frightened by the events, I wanted to cut myself in half, to stay with the children and at the same time go to my husband. No, I had to go and be there for him.

Garry and I arrived outside the magistrates' court. People were sitting around in the evening sun, outside a pub, drinking, laughing and joking. I remember feeling resentful — they were enjoying themselves whilst my world seemed to be falling about my ears.

Men stood around in small groups outside the front of the court building. Garry left the car to ask when the arrested men would appear in court. He was told they should have been heard around four o'clock, but it was near five o'clock and nothing seemed to be happening.

We sat in the car together, making small talk, occasionally switching on the car radio to catch the news bulletins. Time passed just as slowly as it had during the day; six o'clock, then seven o'clock. During this time more people joined the group. We got out to stretch our legs and join them.

One heartwarming moment happened somewhere around 7.30 pm. To the left of the courthouse a pub stood on the corner, separated by a narrow road which ran round behind the court building.

The landlord came out with trays of food — sandwiches and sausage rolls. The men surged forward, some of them — including myself — hadn't eaten for hours. A Welshman's voice called out, 'Now lads, ladies first.' The men stopped and made a gap so that the tray could come to me and to another lady who stood nearby.

It was such a strange feeling, standing in the middle of a pavement, munching sandwiches in a large crowd of men. Listening to them speaking, I could hear different accents, some I recognised — Welsh, Scots — some I couldn't place at all. Like I said, quite an experience. I don't know what time the police put in an appearance, but they came out of a door at the side of the court, so everyone surged to the gate there. I slowly wriggled my way to the front, I was determined Don would see me and know I was there. More hours ticked slowly by, Garry or I leaving briefly to phone home to keep Mum and the children informed. Somewhere around ten o'clock the crowd became restless and a rumour began to circulate that no one would be allowed in the public gallery. Someone had accidentally 'lost' the key. The mood became tense and some of the men began to get annoyed. This after all was Britain, and it was the law for the public to have access — wasn't it?

I went to phone Sheffield Police Station to try to find out what was happening. They couldn't lock the men up without a trial — could they?

I couldn't believe it when the police officer answered that they hadn't got anyone of that name. I didn't know what to do, what to think. I ran back to Garry to tell him — a man standing nearby overheard me — he was the owner of the voice I had heard earlier reminding the crowd 'ladies first'. He was in his fifties and had the same quiet, calm attitude that my father had; in fact he reminded me a great deal of my old dad. He said, 'They've probably transferred him and things are so hectic they won't know who they've got or what's going on. Don't worry love, he'll be all right.'

After a while I noticed a slightly-built lady weaving in and out of the crowd. People were stopping her to ask questions. A whisper went round the crowd that she was a solicitor sent on behalf of the NUM. As she came closer and was about to pass me, I also stopped her and asked if she had seen my husband, describing him as briefly as possible. I was really anxious by this time and I suppose she could see that for herself. She stopped and gave me all her attention.

'I'll try to make enquiries when I go back to Rotherham Police Station, but it is terrible down there. There are as many as ten men in a one-man cell. Some are badly injured and one seems to be unconscious, or in a coma.' As she was about to leave I asked her about being allowed in court and went on to tell her about the 'lost' key. She checked her step, turned around and headed off back to the courthouse. I saw her reappear and skirt the crowd this time, going back towards the police station. Shortly afterwards a man came running from behind the court building and shouted that the door to the gallery was open. Miraculously the key had materialised and hadn't been lost after all. The men around made a great deal of this, shouting to the police officers standing around. I must admit they did go over the top making an issue of it, but I could understand the reason why. The conversation all around me changed and earnest discussions went on about what they thought of the police and how everyone felt that their trust in the police had gone forever.

How much later the mobile prison vehicles started to arrive, I haven't a clue. I was tired, hungry, and really dispirited by that time. A little earlier a senior police officer had appeared with a walkie-talkie and began to send messages. Being quite near, I heard him saying there were a lot of pickets outside the courtroom and to go round again. It slowly sank into my head, which was throbbing by this time, that I was a picket. Despite everything I found this extremely funny — my image of pickets were big fellows, flat caps, standing around an open barrier. Did I really look like a picket: cream suit, pale blue blouse with frills around the neck, and high-heeled strappy sandals? Cor! I think he must have had something wrong with his eyes.

Soon afterwards, the mobile police cells drove up in relays. Ten men at a time left with handcuffs on, attached to a police officer. After what seemed like hours, Don finally came out of a vehicle. I think perhaps seven lots of men had disembarked by this time. Don saw me almost at the same instant I saw him. Different emotions flitted across his face — astonishment, then concern, and after a quick grin he was rushed away into the courtroom. I had just enough time to say I would meet him outside this gate afterwards. I had my fingers crossed during the time I said this, because I was fully aware he might not leave with me. It also made me aware that we never really get out of using childish gestures in time of trouble. I remember thinking that the only prisoners I had seen before had been on television and they usually had blankets or coats thrown over their heads. I grinned to myself thinking of Don like that.

After the police vehicle drove off again, I asked the police officers standing in line along the pavement if they would please excuse me and let me through to go to the gallery. The policewoman barring my way spun round and pushed her face almost into mine, and said very nastily that I could go, but she was going to be watching me. I was flabbergasted by this, I didn't know what to make of it. If I had been rude, abusive or aggressive I would have understood it, but I wasn't.

I hurried off, almost running past the other officers and the crowd, quite forgetting Garry in the process. I was going up the steps when I realised he was behind me and stopped to wait. He asked what the policewoman had said and I told him briefly, but it had rattled me more than I wanted to admit to him.

I sat on the rock-hard wooden seat for another hour, while the gallery filled up around me. Some people stood at the back and spilled out into the entrance area. People came and went in the courtroom below. The lady I had spoken to earlier came into the courtroom and went into an intense conversation with two men already in the room. After a while the meeting broke up and she vanished again, only to reappear at intervals.

At one point she noticed me sitting on the front seat. She came over and stood beneath me. She quietly asked if I had any news of the whereabouts of my husband. After answering her I thanked her, and with a quick smile she disappeared again. Sometimes, thinking back to that day, I recall her kindness in remembering me when she was so obviously overworked, and tired like the rest of us.

A few minutes later the court below became busy. Men walked into the courtroom from a door I couldn't see, but came into view as they began to file into the benches running down the left-hand side of the courtroom. It became clear that they were to have their hearing en masse, not, like I thought, individually in the dock. Each was approached individually and asked if they were Mr Smith or whatever name they were, and if they lived at the address which was written on the paper they were reading from. The men were then addressed in smaller groups of three or four, had the charges read against them, and finally bailed to appear at the court at a later date. Many of the groups came and went during my vigil. I only recognised one other person who appeared that night. He was the NUM Treasurer, Dougie Robertson. I had met him during my time in the action group. He seemed to be as pleased as Don to see me there. He looked up, smiled and gave me the 'thumbs up' sign.

Don finally appeared sometime around one o'clock in the morning. I felt by this time that my head would explode with tension. I think it was because I had begun to think that the ones with the most serious charges would appear last. I was right, but Don wasn't one of them. He was charged with breaching the peace and threatening behaviour. Eventually he was free to go home.

Garry and I stood up to leave between the next hearing and Don leaving the courtroom. The Welshman and his friends stood up and came over to say goodbye, and wished me and my family the best of luck.

We met Don outside the gate as promised and it wasn't like in films, the big reunion bit. Just a quick peck on the cheek, because any more than that would have embarrassed him to death, especially in front of the small crowd hanging round still. During the drive home Don told us what had really happened, but first let me say why I never believed he had done anything wrong. The first reason: he had promised that never would he do anything to jeopardise his jobs because our entire livelihood depended on them. By getting into trouble it would mean hurting me and the children. The second reason takes me back in time to his army career — he had been in riots before, in Londonderry, and had seen the real effect of stone-throwing. He was on the streets with his mates, being petrol bombed and stoned when some instinct made him duck. Unfortunately his mate Chad, didn't. On turning round Don found him lying on the ground with his eye gouged out of his head. That had the most profound effect. Never, never would he throw anything, so, even if one hundred police officers swore on one hundred Bibles, I would know they would be lying, because that day never fades in Don's memory.

Don had been sent to picket Orgreave coking plant again. He had been on several previous occasions. The aim being to attempt to talk to the lorry drivers and persuade them to discontinue the delivery of coke to the steel works. Two separate convoys comprising twenty to thirty empty lorries would descend on to the coking plant. One in the morning and one in the afternoon to load up with coke in order to keep the steel production rolling.

There had been the usual pushing and shouting, but not much violence. Occasionally some idiot would throw something, and the police were quick to react, running out to grab a man or two. It didn't mean they actually caught the culprits, because they would grab anyone. Well, they had to show they were doing their job! By arresting them and sending them through to the courts it cut down on the men able to go picketing because invariably the conditions of bail would be that they weren't to go to any property owned by the NCB, BSC or CEGB.

This picket was different, however, because right from the start it became obvious that it was to be a real mass picket. Thousands of men began to arrive from early in the morning, from all over the British Isles — Wales, Kent and as far away as Scotland. Initially everyone was good-natured, until the coke wagons with the mesh grills covering the windows thundered through.

The now ritual chanting started. The police had no intention of letting anyone near the entrance of the coking plant to reason with the drivers. Just the opposite. It was as if the arrival of the wagons was a cue for the police to charge and disperse the pickets from all directions. All hell broke loose! In that particular area in which Don stood, police charged from the edge of the field on Poplar Way to disperse the pickets. Fights broke out, police battering pickets, pickets retaliating with stones, fists etc. Scared men began fleeing, running anywhere, everywhere, nowhere, unable to escape from the menacing sight of mounted police charging towards them. Batons held high to come smashing down on the unprotected heads of boys and men.

Don saw such mindless, sickening and outrageous acts during this period that the scenes of violence he had witnessed during his stints in Northern Ireland were superseded by the atrocities he was witnessing by, of all people, the police.

Don and a few friends took refuge on a small banking. Men gathered beside and behind him in a very short space of time. Fury emanated from the crowd. (Don told me that he had never felt such blind absolute rage as he felt during those few minutes.) As the men surged forward Don was literally thrown into the police standing in front of him. Everything happened very quick, as he felt himself falling he saw a silver-grey-haired inspector reach out towards him. During those briefest of seconds Don thought, it's my turn for a thorough beating. He felt pain in his head as the inspector grabbed hold of his hair to carry on the momentum of pulling him to the ground among the other police officers' legs and feet. He struggled to his feet full of rage, yelled at the inspector, 'What did you do that for, you bastard!' and carried on foolishly to say, 'I'll have you for that!' Straight away four or five police officers jumped on him and pummelled him to the ground, some putting their boot in for good measure. Eventually one of the officers grabbed him by the leg, another by his left arm, and dragged him into a clearing behind the police line. Don tried to regain his balance. One of the officers let go of his leg and got him around the neck in a headlock, splitting his mouth open in doing so. He began to struggle really hard because he couldn't breathe and felt he was about to become unconscious. The officer realised he was exerting too much pressure and that Don was in great distress. After releasing him a little he asked if he would calm down if he let go. Obviously Don was only too willing. He was led away to a private bus which had brought in the officers. He was thrown bodily on board and the next thing he remembered was looking up from where he was sprawled, half way on the steps and passage in front of the driver's seat, to see Dougie Robertson, the NUM Treasurer from his own pit. Don said something like 'Thank God for a friendly face.' He was then ushered to a passenger seat opposite Dougie and handcuffed to a sort of handrail below the window. Minutes later they came to confiscate everything in his pockets — better them than me! My husband has pockets like a dustbin — sweet wrappers from the children, to name just some.

One of the police officers sank down in the seat next to Don's and offered him a cigarette and a can of pineapple juice. They sat together for quite a while, talking in turn about their families, both glad to be away from the mayhem going on outside. That was until a senior police officer strutted on board. Don didn't know what rank he was but it must have been quite high because of the pips and braiding. He marched up and down the bus jeering at the handcuffed men — quite a few men had been taken on board during the peaceful minutes the two men had been together. This officer wanted to know if Scargill was worth it, and did they think it worth it to be martyrs for an idiot like him.

After perhaps an hour to an hour and a half sitting on board the bus, they were driven to Sheffield Police Station and charged with disturbing the peace and threatening behaviour. Don's belt and shoes were removed, the shoes being left outside the cell door. The room he found himself in was three yards by two yards. A cubicle stood in the corner containing a toilet. There was a window made up of small panes of very thick frosted glass. Along the wall facing the door was a hard wooden bed. Don was alone in the cell for perhaps ten minutes, then the door opened and another man was locked in with him. His name was Paul and he came from Thurcroft Pit. He worked on the pit top as a welder. He had been charged with the same offences.

They spent the whole day together with only one or two interruptions. The first around eleven-twenty that morning when Don asked if he could phone home because he had to notify the fire station to take him off call. The second was one o'clock when a meal was brought in. This consisted of twelve baked beans each with a slice of corned beef which had been cut so thinly it looked more like a frilly curtain, and cold powdered potatoes, washed down with a mug of tea. Don has quite a sense of humour — I call it sick at times — and had found the ideal cellmate in Paul. They amused themselves by exchanging jokes and got into a right argument about who was going to have the one baked bean lying on the floor between them. Some time later that day they were taken out of the cell to be finger-printed and photographed. Around five-thirty they were taken out of the cell and put aboard a prison bus to be transferred to Rotherham Police Station. On arrival, they were put in a holding room which contained a desk where a police sergeant sat the entire time. The place was newly built but the air conditioning wasn't working. The room became stifling with all the men crammed into it. Shortly afterwards a small woman entered the room. She was a solicitor representing the NUM (the lady I had spoken to earlier). She set about having the men moved into the exercise yard because some were fainting due to the heat. Many were injured, with nasty gashes to their heads. The men held at Sheffield Police Station didn't have the injuries the men held at Rotherham had. The woman, Gareth Pearce, found a badly injured man barely breathing and unconscious, with congealed blood on his face. He had been thrown on one of the wooden beds and left there for quite some time before she saw him. No animal would have been that badly treated; police dogs and horses were treated like royalty compared to the men, but then they were miners, weren't they. Most of the men arrested that day wore only jeans and T-shirts which didn't give any protection against the crack of the truncheons. Don actually saw the badly injured man and others with massive bruising and gashes on the backs of their heads as he was moved down the corridors to the coolness of the exercise yard. Don's brief 'freedom' of the exercise yard proved to be a great relief. The chance to talk to other mates as well as Paul his cell mate. The chance to have a cigarette, and more importantly the fresh air. By the time he arrived in the exercise yard a lot of his mates were there. Some sitting, some standing, others lying down on the yard floor totally exhausted by the day's events. Along with the men he knew were colleagues from other coal fields. Scottish, Welsh, Geordies as well as other Yorkshire lads.

Don tried to comfort one very young Scottish lad who was continually close to tears through worry about how to inform his young wife and his mother.

Looking around the exercise yard, the sight of the men with congealed blood on their faces and heads, stains of grass, blood and sweat on their torn and ripped clothing was reminiscent of some old portrait, the aftermath of the hand-to-hand fighting of battles in years gone by. This wasn't a painting, this was for real. These men were feeling the after-effects of the blows — bruising, gashes, broken limbs. They were shocked and bewildered by the day's events. The reality of it all not quite sinking in.

After a couple of hours of talking to old and new friends and the solicitor, Gareth Pearce, they were all informed that they were to be transported to Rotherham Magistrates Court.

Two at a time, they were handcuffed to a police officer and taken to a police bus where they were locked in separate, solid, metal cells, measuring two feet six inches square. Don couldn't sit down on the narrow wooden seat because of his size, so he spent the journey — some eight to ten miles — to Rotherham standing up. Most of the men did. By peering through the small, barred opening in the door he could just glimpse two or three more cell doors and their inhabitants peering back at him. The general conversation and banter was jokey and light-hearted with the occasional insult directed at the stony-faced police escort seated at the rear end of the bus.

The light-heartedness was just a cover-up. All the men knew how serious the situation was, but no way would any police officer get them down. They might be penniless, they might be injured, but these police officers would not and could not take away the humour and comradeship these men held like some kind of invisible shield which somehow gave strength and determination to see them through all that had happened and was in store for them.

On arrival at the courthouse in Rotherham the thing which sticks out in his mind the most was the chanting from the considerable crowd now gathered there of friends, relatives and general NUM supporters.

It was a matter of a few yards from alighting from the bus to actually entering the courthouse, handcuffed yet again to a police officer. In this short space of time he caught sight of me in the crowd. He remembers being totally shocked at seeing me there, especially as it it was around eleven o'clock at night. All he could think about was who was looking after Nikki and Darren and how did she (I) get there? How would we get home? More to the point how would she get home again, safely, if I wasn't released on bail?

Don had already been told earlier by Gareth Pearce that possibly six or more men would not get bail, and that proved to be the case.

Don was taken with the remainder of the accused to the cells beneath the courthouse, where they were placed a dozen or so to a cell whilst the proceedings got under way. This building was a total contrast to the modern one at Sheffield. It was old, unkempt with a dank smell which lingered in the air as the various legal representatives flitted from cell to cell gaining information.

Eventually they were led up into the courthouse proper, in groups of sixteen or so. Don was surprised, then alarmed at the prospect of being 'tried' en masse. Was this going to be some kind of judicial sham (his words) or was he going to get a fair hearing in his own right? The burden of the charge hanging over him became heavier by the minute. What was he doing here? he kept asking himself. It must be some kind of dream. It wasn't. It was Don's turn to be confronted by the magistrate. His name and address were read to which he replied, 'Correct.' Then they read the charge to which he replied that he understood. Finally he was released on bail with, however, certain restrictions to be adhered to. The conditions were that he was not to go within one mile of the Orgreave coking plant, also not to attend any premises of the NCB, British Steel Corporation or Central Electricity Generating Board other than his own place of employment.

He was discharged and told to appear at a later date. After being ushered out of the court room he said goodbye to Paul (he was to meet up with him again at the subsequent court hearings and socially one year later at a social evening marking the advent of the final court case when all the men were acquitted). Then he hurried off to find me. He was surprised and relieved to see that I hadn't been alone, that Garry had been with me all the time. We were all subdued during the drive back to our home.

Mum came out to meet us after hearing the car pull up. It was sometime after two o'clock in the morning, so she obviously wanted to be on her way home. After a quick 'thank you' she was driven home by Garry. He also wanted to get home as he had to get up for work himself the next morning, or should I say, later that same morning.

Both children had fallen asleep downstairs waiting for us. Darren was lying in a ball on the settee, half undressed. His face was puffy and dirty marks showed he had been crying before falling asleep. Nikki was asleep on the floor. I gently shook her awake, it took her a few minutes to realise where she was, and why she wasn't in bed. She threw herself into Don's arms and clung on to him as though if she let go he would disappear again. Don carried Darren up to bed while I walked behind Nikki to make sure she didn't fall. She was tired and very unsteady. We tucked them up and kissed them goodnight. The minutes that followed were pretty personal, so I'm not going into detail — it is sufficient to say that it was nice to be together again. After preparing something to eat we finally fell into bed, not to sleep though — we talked until daybreak about what we thought the consequences would be. Not ever having had anything to do with the law we really didn't have any idea.

Darren was absolutely ecstatic that his Dad was home. We didn't discuss what had happened, especially about the police, in front of him. Darren really had developed a deep hatred of the police and we had to do everything we could to stop it getting any worse.

The bulletins gave us the news that ninety-five men had been arrested at Orgreave, four of these were now in Armley Jail in Leeds. Politicians were out for blood, and I don't think it mattered whether the men arrested were guilty or not, as long as it looked as if the culprits had been imprisoned.

They had been widely televised, hadn't they? And it seemed to be quite immaterial that most of the men had been arrested prior to the footage being shot. They had been in prison cells during this time. Don was actually arrested at 9.30 in the morning. Most of the violence happened around 11.30 when the second convoy of wagons went into the coking plant. We knew without doubt that Don and the other men would be condemned and judged by those television shots. How on earth do you prove you are innocent when you are already presumed guilty in advance?

Our worry was quite justified when Don returned to court two weeks later. He was then charged with Unlawful Assembly. He was one of the lucky eleven, the other eighty-two men arrested that day had riot charges brought against them. Not all at once I might add, just a few at each court hearing. Don elected, like the others, to have his case heard at Crown Court, hopefully to have a fair hearing, so that he could at least give an account of the day. We even doubted that they would indeed have a fair hearing. After all, juries are made up of television viewers, aren't they? They had seen the 'truth' on the videos taken by the media and the 'facts' spoke for themselves. One long and worrying year was to pass before Don's trial came to court.

CHAPTER SIX

Pride

'Apply to the Parish Council for help'

After being arrested Don couldn't go 'flying picketing', so he picketed at the end of Cortonwood Lane. This had been called the 'Alamo', (from an incident in the war between the USA and Mexico, when there was a fight to the last man by an American unit) — an unfortunate name really.

Sometimes the children and I would go to see him, which would result in some kind of game being played, football being the favourite. Men and boys alike would play around, more and more would join in until eventually the boys would drop out and only the men would stay. Most of them, being clowns, would play up to the crowd so by the time they had finished fooling around, most of the audience would have 'stitch'. These times were such good fun, and happened when neither police nor television crews were around!

Realising that the strike would most probably run into the winter, Don began to think about fuel to keep the children warm. Dad told him about a field in Brampton where once a coke stockpile had been. Both of them started going there, and I went along once or twice, but it broke my heart to see them grovelling on the ground digging, sometimes with their bare hands, to find the coke hidden beneath the soil and grass. But it was watching Dad which shattered me most. The many years he had spent underground had taken their toll of him over the years. The big strapping man I remembered had changed into a man old before his time. The last few years had seen him develop a terrible bronchial cough. The coughing bouts would rack his entire frame, sometimes bringing on asthma attacks. I would watch him do his level best to bag a few coke lumps, then another attack would take over, perhaps lasting up to ten minutes. Dear God, how it hurt to see him like that, but the real ordeal was to come. To reach his home in Wombwell he would have to climb over a wall with his bike, tie the small bag of coke onto the back of the bike, and either push it or try to ride it home. It was two and a half miles between the field and his house, with two or three steep hills to climb first. Don helped of course, as much as he could. He would carry his own sack a few yards then run back to take a turn with the bike. With Don being on call to the fire station he couldn't leave the immediate area, so sometimes I would walk Dad to the Alamo. I would watch him struggle with the wretched bike, having to stop each time a coughing bout took hold of him. I had tears in my eyes and such an enormous lump in my throat that I could barely speak. Before he would finally disappear from sight he would turn to give me a wave. How I loved that man and his stubborn independence; he would never let me help him. It was man's work and no daughter of his would carry coke. Many times he would virtually collapse when he reached home. Ash-grey, so ill that he couldn't catch his breath. Mum and I began to think, at the back of our minds, that each trip would be his last one. But there was no way he could be persuaded not to go: he had provided for his family all his married life and that was not going to change.

Dad also did his share of picketing at his pit, Darfield Main. Luckily if there seemed to be any trouble brewing, either an NUM person, or sometimes a police officer would go up to him and say it was probably time he went off home. I think everyone could see he wasn't fit to run away from trouble and I thank them from the bottom of my heart for their concern and care and making sure he was safe.

Don changed during the weeks that followed his arrest. Worry was one of the reasons, but his family down in Nottingham began to get in touch less and less and it preyed on his mind. Any phone calls made between us became more and more strained and difficult and were usually taken up by us listening to their opinions of Scargill and the strike. We didn't want Don's parents or family to take sides, only to understand just a little that we were fighting for our livelihood. Jobs are harder to find in mining communities than in large textile cities like Nottingham. We didn't want or ask for any financial help ever, all we wanted was a little understanding. Don became withdrawn and distant, even from me. He felt abandoned by his own family. He had always been there for them in times of crisis, sometimes financially, but always to give moral support. This, the first and only time he had ever wanted or needed support, it just wasn't there. Not one of his family cared enough to give him even a little, and this affected him deeply.

John, Don's younger brother, who had lived with us for a few months after his demob from the army, still lived locally in the next town of Wombwell. Since leaving us, some five or six years earlier, he had married a local girl and settled down to family life.

He was not, however, involved in the strike as he worked as a bus driver for the Yorkshire Traction Company. Don and John didn't see much of each other before the strike, only on rare occasions. This was mainly due to both of them working unsocial hours at their respective places of work.

On the odd occasion that I saw John, especially during this particularly worrying time, he would make inane remarks about how the strike had changed Don. It took a great deal of self-control not to yell at him that it was his family that had changed him, not the strike.

I tried everything I could, first trying to show Don my love by being more affectionate. He rebuffed me, usually snarling that he was all right and wanted to be left alone. He wouldn't talk to me, let alone discuss his feelings. I tried so hard to show him I was still there and that I had backed everything he had done during the strike. He didn't even want to know me and put a large icy wall up between us. He would silently go up to bed quite deliberately before me, to turn his back without so much as a 'goodnight'. He didn't sleep though, because he would toss and turn for hours before getting up again. I had never felt so lonely and alone in our entire marriage. He became gaunt in the face and lost a lot of weight, which, already being slightly built, he couldn't afford to lose.

Don came out of it quite a few weeks later, but his attitude towards his family and a lot of other things changed drastically during this time. The relationship between us went back to normal, but had changed to a somehow deeper level, as if he saw me differently. I was glad to see him finally pull himself out of his own particular hell.

The summer came and went, along with our hopes of some kind of settlement. First hope, then a breakdown in negotiations. Hope upon hope, dashed time after time.

Finances became harder and harder as the bills came in to be paid. Don went to the food kitchens only very occasionally. I only went once because I felt I was taking food from people worse off than myself, and there were plenty of them.

As time went on our children became desperate for socks and shoes. Sue, our next-door neighbour, told me, 'Apply to the Parish Council for help.' She and most of the miners' families in the village had had £10 vouchers to help out. I applied, after a lot of pressure from Sue, and did receive some money. During the summer months the Parish Council bought plimsolls for most of the village children, and when winter started in earnest I also applied for winter coats from the Education Authority. It wasn't easy going to fetch them. I hated it, but I had to hide my own distaste for applying for the necessary things needed for Nikki and Darren. It seemed so important to me that Don shouldn't do this kind of thing. I was determined he wouldn't lose his pride, no matter how long the strike lasted.

CHAPTER SEVEN

They Cared
'I want you to take this'

We learnt a very valuable lesson during that long year. Other people's warm-hearted generosity and kindness has stayed with me even to this day.

Sometime in May I was on my way home from work when I met Dee Mitchell, a childhood friend of mine (she and her family had moved into the adjoining council house when she was five years and I was two years old.)

She asked how Don and I were coping and if my parents were all right. I told her briefly but didn't go into too much detail. A day or so later she arrived at my home unannounced. There was nothing strange about that, because we have a unique friendship where we may not see each other for weeks, months, even years, then meet again and carry on as if we had said goodbye the night before.

Dee handed me two carrier bags full of food — bread, milk, eggs and potatoes. I refused to take them at first, she had two children of her own — Nicola (9) and Scott (7) — to feed and clothe. 'Jackie, take it. You would help me if I was in the same situation — do shut up and go put the kettle on.' At least doing that small job gave me enough time to stop the tears.

Dee and her children visited about once a month from then on, which I appreciated — she's more like a sister I never had, than a friend. I knew she made time to visit me in her very busy life of looking after her family, helping her husband in his new business venture, and visiting her disabled mother three times each week. So it wasn't just the gift of the food and sweets for my children I appreciated, it was everything that entailed, the time, the money, and most of all the thought.

Another act of kindness happened in August. Don was walking around Barnsley, trying to find a toy shop which sold Transformers. These toys had been widely advertised, but hadn't reached many toy shops. It was near to Darren's tenth birthday and we had cut down even more to be able to afford one toy for him, around £5. Darren had set his heart on one particular model, and didn't want a toy which was very similar which was readily available, so Don was trekking from store to store trying to find one. He bumped into Frank, a full-time fireman who worked on 'Blue Watch' at Brampton Fire Station. Don asked him if he knew of any more stores to try. After a pleasant exchange of conversation, Don tried the shops Frank had suggested, and did in fact find one.

It was the morning of Darren's birthday, Don was out and the children were still in bed, because it was school holidays. I had only been up a short time when I heard knocking at the back door. Realising I was only in my dressing gown, I peered round the door, to see a man I had previously seen at the fire station. He gave me an envelope and said their Watch had had a collection, and would we give this to Darren for his birthday. I just didn't know what to say. I somehow managed a quick 'Thank you' before he vanished down the path. I stood with my back to the door, tears streaming down my face. I can't remember the exact amount of money — I think it was £10, but it wasn't the actual gift, it was that these people, some I didn't even know personally, had thought about us enough to go to the trouble of actually collecting money for our son's birthday. I knew I was an idiot for crying but their kindness affected me deeply, especially as it had been so unexpected.

All the other acts of kindness meant a great deal to me but the one that stays in my memory is unique because it came so unexpectedly, and from a complete stranger who lived miles away, somewhere near London.

A group of representatives from the Fire Brigade's Union had come to Brampton to find out for themselves just how the strike was affecting the ordinary people living in a mining community.

The representatives had arranged an evening out for anyone from the mining community to join them in Cortonwood's Welfare Club. The Club had been in existence, in one form or another, since the mine first opened. (The Welfare served as a social meeting place for the miners and their families; the miners helped with the up-keep by paying weekly contributions, deducted from their wages.) We had been asked by some of Brampton Fire Station's full-time firemen if we were going once or twice during that day. We decided not to go, because we only had enough money for my fares to work, and felt it quite inappropriate to go out and expect other people to pay for our drinks.

At nine o'clock we had a phone call asking us to go up to meet some of the men who had travelled all the way from near London. We refused but thanked them for the invitation. The phone rang again, this time it was Cyril Webb, the FBU representative from Brampton station. To say that he was a little irate is quite an understatement. We were told, or should I say, Don was told that he was the most stubborn, pig-headed, independent and stupid person Cyril had ever met. We were to come up to the club pronto or he was going to come down and tell us exactly what he thought of our stubbornness. We eventually decided, OK, we would go to keep the peace, have one drink, then come back home.

It didn't turn out like that at all. On entering the room we were warmly greeted by Cyril and the other men from the fire station. We were introduced to some of the visitors who were circulating the room, meeting people. One gentleman stayed to chat (sadly I have forgotten his name); he was so genuine in his concern. A table finally became vacant, so we decided to have just one more drink, then go home. Cyril and the others had no intention of letting us go. After they found out what we were drinking we would be only half way down the glass when another one would appear. The man stayed talking to me all night, asking about how we were coping and about Nikki and Darren. I skipped over our problems. I wanted him to know about the people who knew what real poverty was like — the single miners who had not had so much as a penny since the strike began in March.

It was closing time and everyone was saying goodbye. Don and quite a few of the men were a little worse for wear, including the gentleman I had spent the evening talking to. As I was leaving he came up to me to give me a quick hug and a kiss on the cheek. 'Jackie, I want you to take this and buy your kids a bit of something for Christmas,' he said, pushing some money into my hand. I looked down to see two ten-pound notes screwed up in my hand. I wouldn't accept it and it wasn't until he saw how upset I was that he stopped insisting. I just couldn't take money from someone who had been kind and concerned. It was enough that he had taken the trouble to find out about the people of Brampton. He cared, and that was enough. We parted company, never to meet again, but somehow it made the hardship of the strike a little easier to bear knowing that not everyone condemned us for striking to try to save jobs.

A few days before Christmas, a letter arrived postmarked Hampshire. I opened it to find a photocopy of an advertisement for a circus, folded inside were two ten-pound notes. No letter, nothing to say who had sent it. I'll never know for sure, but in my heart of hearts I believe it was that FBU representative, and even now not a week goes by without me remembering his kindness, and all the other people who cared. That man must have gone to the trouble of finding out our surname, as well as the address, and that is what means the most. I'll never be able to thank him and obviously he didn't want my thanks, it must have been enough for him to have helped.

CHAPTER EIGHT

Laughter
'Save me from her and her blackberries'

Up to now my memories seem to be sad, bad or serious, but laughter was an integral part of the strike. You either laughed or cried! Laughter is harder to write about because 'funny' moments are hard to capture unless you're there to witness them.

One of our funny moments stays in my memory because just for once I actually 'won' one of the skirmishes between Don and myself.

During a trip to the coke field Don and Dad went to, I noticed bushes full of blackberries, subsequently I gathered quite a few. We have two apple trees, so I was able to make puddings quite cheaply and apparently far too often.

Don had been gardening and on entering the kitchen he saw me with the container filled with the remaining blackberries I had frozen. Sinking to the floor, he went on his knees and put his hands together in prayer, and said, 'Dear God, no more — I won't ever ask for anything else if you will only save me from her and her blackberries.'

I replied with something like 'I'll have you know Cordon Bleu's got nothing on my cuisine; how many wives go to the trouble I do? Apple pies, sometimes a crumble, and the most delicious of all, Fruit Charlotte. I even go to the trouble of reversing the blackberries and apple in turn. So what have you to be so picky about? Besides, the modern-day thinking is that fibre's good for you!'

'I've been sitting on the toilet for the last two weeks, so don't talk about fibre,' he responded. 'Ten pounds of blackberries each meal is just a little too much!' (Don never exaggerates!)

'Look at that,' he said, sticking out his tongue and trying to peer down his nose to see it, 'In your case Cordon Bleu is more that Cordon Blue.' Then he held out his hands, which were filthy from weeding the garden, and went on to say, 'God! Look what you've done to me, my hands are black, even my...' I immediately cut him off, he's so unpredictable or should I say, predictable, and always takes great delight in deliberately trying to make me blush. I wasn't about to oblige him this time.

'All right, all right, I get the message, you'd prefer arsenic on toast for tea.' He finally removed himself from under my feet, but not without having the last laugh, he thought. He went out of the door, closing it behind him, only to open it again to pop his head round the door. 'By the way,' he said, 'I was only going to say I had black feet as well!' He just managed to disappear again before the soggy dishcloth hit the door where his head had been. I could hear him laughing all the way to the top of the garden. Drat the man, he always manages to win.

Deciding to be the sweet, kind-hearted wife that I am, I took him a nice hot steaming mug of tea, quite forgetting that I had salted instead of sugared! I can't tell you how much satisfaction I got out of standing at the kitchen window to watch him take his first, and only, mouthful. Revenge they say is sweet, sometimes it can be salty as well!

Another of our 'funny' moments was also about food. Don came home from the fire station one day, and walking into the house, said 'Cor, something smells nice.' I was boiling some bones in a saucepan to make stock for the stew for the evening meal. I said, 'Oh it's only some bones for the dog.' He came up behind me (I was standing preparing vegetables for the stew). He turned me round and put his hand across my forehead.

'Are you sure you're feeling all right? I hate to tell you this, but we DON'T HAVE A DOG.' Pushing him away I said, 'I know, but it's less embarrassing to ask at the butchers for bones for the dog. I only hope he doesn't find out I haven't got one.'

He turned around and began to tiptoe out of the kitchen in a very exaggerated fashion, like in the cartoons. On his reaching the front door I asked him where he was going — stupid question really. 'I'm going to see someone . . . the butcher.' I ran to the door only to see him going round the bend in the road. I'm going to kill that man one of these days; I found out that he really did go to the shop.

Half an hour or so later I dished up tea, stew for the children and myself. You should have seen Don's face when I placed the plate of bones in front of him. But as usual he had to have the last laugh. The next thing I knew he was on the floor, on all fours, wagging his rear end and barking. The children were in hysterics when he bit my ankles and my bottom sticking out between the back rest and the seat of the chair. One of these days . . .

CHAPTER NINE

Division
'Don't they love us any more?'

The contact between Don's family and us gradually became more and more distant. I don't know how they thought we were managing, they didn't ask and we never said. One thing which really hurt us was that they didn't get in touch with Nikki and Darren as they had always done previously. The usual visit to their grandparents in Nottingham at Spring Bank didn't materialise either. The children couldn't understand why Grandma and Grandad Albert didn't want them any more.

Don became angrier and angrier about them having this attitude. OK, it was all right to have a different opinion from us, we understood that, but the children weren't to blame for our stand in the strike. One day we were discussing it and, unknown to us, Nikki had come home from school and overheard us.

'Why are you mad at Grandma and Grandad? I still love them and Carol,' this was Don's sister, still living at home. 'Don't they love us any more?' She began to cry. I went to put my arms around her but she shrugged me off and ran upstairs to her bedroom. What on earth do you say? I went up to try to explain that sometimes adults have disagreements and that was what was happening right now because of the strike. She said that she hadn't had a 'disagreement' so why didn't Grandma phone her like before. Shortly afterwards they rang to say they had cancelled Carol's twenty-first birthday party because it would be terrible for all concerned if Richard (the working miner), Sandra and family went to the party along with ourselves. It wouldn't be fair if a row broke out and spoiled the celebration. We told them it was highly unlikely that we could afford the travel expenses so we wouldn't be there to spoil anything.

The night before Carol's birthday, John came to the house and asked if we had a present and card to take down to the party. First, we were astonished that he actually thought we had any money for presents — sometimes we found it hard just to eat. Secondly, the party had been cancelled, hadn't it? They had just moved the venue, not cancelled it, but didn't bother to tell us. The thing that hurt us most was that Nikki and Darren hadn't been asked to go. John went down in a car so could have taken them quite easily. They were punishing our children for us and that hurt. Even if they couldn't have gone in the car we would have found some way to find the five-pounds travel expenses for them to be put on a coach, as before.

Don became even more bitter during the holiday months. His parents had phoned to say that Gran, Albert's mother, had been taken ill and Sandra was going on holiday in her place. Nothing wrong with that, but it was them saying that they would have asked me to go with them, but as we were so obviously short of money, I wouldn't have been able to pay my way. The hurt had gone deep with Don. There had been no need to even mention it, because we were miles away and wouldn't have been any the wiser about Sandra going with them.

One day John came to visit us to give us a message that Mum and Albert would never ring us again or get in touch if we didn't get in touch with them first. To be honest we hadn't phoned much. One reason was the phone bill, this became harder and harder to pay. The second reason was that listening to their opinions became more difficult to take, so it was easier not to phone in the first place than to have an outright confrontation. But I had an uneasy feeling there was more going on that I couldn't see.

Don was adamant he would never ring, never again. He hadn't abandoned them, they were abandoning us. When I told him that I would ring, he said that I could 'please myself' but I was not to involve him. I phoned, but it was terrible, the atmosphere was frosty and I had to really work hard to make conversation and it only became slightly easier towards the end of the call.

Don couldn't understand why I had 'lowered my pride' like that. He just didn't understand that I loved him and if I could try to build bridges between him and his family I would. It hadn't been easy but it would have been silly to have tried to build bridges between the mining community and the media, if I couldn't also do the same within my own family.

Soon afterwards Don's Mum rang to ask if she could visit the children. She stayed three or four days and by the time she went home again things were better between her and Don.

After the visit everything changed . . . I don't know to this day what it was, I guess I'll never know, but they were completely different. They seemed to be genuinely concerned about us and sent us all presents for Christmas, as well as a food parcel and a wine-making kit for Don to make a drink for Christmas.

CHAPTER TEN

Rioting
'They will wreck the place'

The BBC's radio journalist, Triona Holden, who had interviewed Jenny and me, arrived at my home one evening in November accompanied by Jenny. I was extremely surprised because I hadn't had any contact with Triona since May, and Jenny I hadn't seen much of since my departure from the Action Group. I was quite surprised that Triona had even remembered me let alone gone to the trouble of finding my home. She was very interested in how my own family were coping, and how my parents were. I had spoken of them at length during our last meeting. Fortunately for her, and unfortunately for me, she had caught me at a very upsetting and vulnerable time.

Monday of that week had seen some terrible scenes, rioting and violence from police and miners alike. In the early hours of that Monday morning, Jenny burst into my home and asked me to accompany her to her house. She had a badly injured man in her living room. The man had been taken to Jenny's by a local miner, from the scene of the rioting at the top of the street. Jenny's house was three blocks down the road and she always had her door open to anyone who wanted somewhere to take refuge, refreshments, etc.

Don and I went with her (both of us having experience of first aid) to see if we could give assistance. The man had fallen, we can only assume, on to a jagged piece of glass and sustained a terrible gash several inches long, running down his leg from just below his knee. He had lost a lot of blood. I started to administer first aid, but soon realised I would need more dressings. Don took over trying to stem the bleeding as I ran back down the street to Jackie Palfreyman's who had a large first aid box. Her first aid box was pretty comprehensive because of her being a Girl Guide Leader, and she always kept the box fully equipped. Ours, unfortunately, being quite small, had dwindled down and because of the lack of money we hadn't been able to replenish items used out of it. Don went up to where the rioting was going on at the top of Dearne Road, to try to find the man's friends to have him taken off to hospital. It was no good trying to get an ambulance for him because it wouldn't have got through the mayhem.

As I walked back down the road all hell broke out. Men chased by riot police charged down the road and through gardens. There was screaming and yelling going on all around me. One young lad was caught by a couple of officers who were hitting him with batons. The last time I saw him, nine or ten police officers were round him scuffling. I became aware that more policemen were charging towards me. I began to run, I could hear heavy boots getting nearer and nearer. On reaching my gate I glimpsed Nikki's frightened face at the window. I was so terrified by this time, expecting at any moment to be hit on the back of my head, that I was fumbling with the key to open the door for what seemed an eternity. First the key wouldn't go into the lock, then my fingers couldn't turn it. I almost fell through the door, slammed it shut and locked it. I was shaking so much by this time I felt as if my legs had turned to water. Both children came running, Darren from upstairs and Nikki from the living room. 'Where's Dad?' they both asked. Not knowing, I said, 'He'll be coming home soon.' The minutes passed and we all heard the yells and sounds of splintering wood, then all went quiet.

How much longer passed I don't know, but the shouting and loud noises could still be heard. Sirens sounded in the distance.

Then the high-pitched sirens of the police vehicle came closer. We all ran to the window to see the doors of the houses opening. Men of all ages and sizes were running inside. Remembering that youth I had seen, I ran and opened my door too and in quick succession about seventeen men ran into my house. Before any police officers came into sight I slammed and locked the door again, and ran to make sure the back door was also locked. Back in the living room one of the men had the children sitting together on a chair talking to them. Most of the other men were either sitting round the walls or lying on the carpet. 'Come away from the window love,' one said. 'If the police see you with pickets in your house they will wreck the place.' About ten minutes later one of the men looked out of the window and asked if there was a back way out. They left a few minutes later, but the man who had taken care of the children on first entering the house, asked where my husband was. After I answered quietly that I didn't know, and that he was out there somewhere, he said, 'I'm going to listen for you to lock this door. Don't open it for anyone, only your husband, and keep the kids away from the window.' With that he left, but he did wait to make sure I had locked up. They all went over the back fence. Back to the trouble or back home I didn't know. One thing I did know was that the few minutes those miners were in my home I felt safer, and without being told I knew they would have looked after me and the children. I can't say the same for the police—believe me, that takes quite a bit of getting used to.

We all ran to the door when we heard Don's knock (he always knocks in a certain way). I still checked at the window first before unlocking the door. Both children threw their arms around him; hugging them tight he looked at me and asked if I was all right. Untangling himself from the children he gave me a quick hug and began to tell me how he had managed to avoid the police. Some of the men at the back of the crowd were throwing stones so the police charged. Don, having located some of the injured man's friends, was taking them to him when the charge started. Every man ran but Don. Using his army training, he jumped over the wall into the chapel garden, lying very still until it had all gone quiet. If you run, then you draw attention to yourself. He was walking down the road for the second time when the second charge ensued. This time he took cover in Jenny's house, checking on the injured man who was by this time going into shock. Luckily a couple of his friends had taken refuge in her house as well and after the second police charge they quickly fetched the car and took him away to hospital. We didn't hear about the man again, but that injury must have left quite a scar.

Don had just finished telling us all about it when his bleeper suddenly started up. He ran out of the back door shouting to me to lock up and not to let anyone else into the house. The last we saw of him was him vaulting over the back fence.

Don ran through the garages at the back of the houses and out on to the street behind ours, Chapel Avenue. Then he came up to the police cordon across the main street in Brampton, where he was suddenly grabbed. 'Where do you think you're going?' bellowed one of the officers. 'I've just got a fire call,' Don replied, grabbing hold of his bleeper out of his pocket. Finally believing him the officer said 'OK mate, down there,' and pointed him in quite the opposite direction.

'I know the way, I've only been going seven years,' Don yelled back, by this time leaving the police behind and running into no-man's land (the gap between the police and pickets). The sky was full of stones, housebricks and bottles being thrown. Don never knew how he avoided a direct hit, but he managed by zig-zagging those twenty yards. He jumped on the fire tender and they then followed the tender which had already left, manned by full-time firemen. They were putting out the fire, started during the rioting, near to the police cordon. The police then positioned themselves with shields in front, saying they would give them full cover. Getting on with the business of running a hose reel out, Don found this bit about 'taking care' of him highly amusing. One minute he was an enemy, next a hero! After this incident I teased him terribly about being Wurzel Gummidge and whether he had his good or bad 'head' on.

Almost immediately the atmosphere became charged. A man Don knew began to yell, 'Scab, you're nothing but scabs,' and began insulting the firemen near him, saying the fire crew were miners and had scabbed by getting another job. The crowd became very hostile, joining in the chanting of 'Scab!, Scab!' Don suddenly snapped, ran up to the man and grabbed him by the throat, threatening to rearrange his face if he didn't stop exaggerating the situation. Alec Winspear, the sub officer riding the first fire appliance dragged him off and made him get back into the cab of the fire tender and cool down. On returning to the fire station, Don and the other retained crew were called in front of the Divisional Officer. Before the officer could say anything Don owned up to being the one involved in the fracas and said that none of the other men was at all involved. He was carpeted over the incident, but over all the officer was quite understanding though he made no bones about it not happening again.

It wasn't the end of the incident because Don was determined to have it out with this bloke, who suddenly disappeared from the face of the earth and didn't surface again for a couple of weeks. The NUM heard about the trouble and it was brought up at the next Union meeting. It was pointed out that the retained firemen had been doing their job for many years and when the bleepers activate they haven't a clue what the job is, until they are getting on the tender. So the call that day could easily have been to innocent citizens trapped in their homes. Don and the rest of the crew received a round of applause for the work they do and never again did any problems occur, involving them. The man eventually apologised to the fire station and to Don.

The interview Triona recorded of me was taken a couple of days later. Believe me I was still terrified and upset and I came close to breaking down during the interview. Triona started the interview by introducing me and then went on to say that it wasn't the hardship of the strike that I was finding hard to cope with, it was the scenes of violence I had witnessed from the police and pickets alike.

I began by saying that I had had my eyes opened by witnessing the violence from the police officers. Up to that point I had believed them to be the very best in society, and how much I had respected them; that had been the way I had been brought up.

Witnessing the violence had totally changed my opinion of them. Becoming more upset, I said that I didn't think I could believe in them again, ever. I tried to describe how I had seen the police officers charging through people's gardens, kicking in fences as they did so. I told her about tending the injured man and how the police had chased many people, including myself, down Dearne Road and the subsequent beating that young man had sustained. I was almost in tears when I said that the very worst part of it all was that I didn't think anyone outside the mining communities believed that this was truly happening.

I told her that both my children and I were now absolutely terrified of the police. Triona said that during those months of strike I must have hardened myself to all the things I had seen. Would I ever be able to speak to a police officer again? I replied that at that moment in time I wouldn't, I was just too terrified of those people. One minute I could be talking to them, the next, they could return to chasing me again — they had given me nightmares which kept reccuring.

I went on to say: 'For years had anyone heard of trouble in

the mining villages? Now suddenly we were all two-headed monsters — raging animals. Could people in the South really believe that? Surely they must realise something is happening here.'

Triona was upset and disturbed at the change in me and went on to say, 'Six months ago you were a lot calmer a person than you are now about the whole thing.'

I replied, 'Yes, I was, but now I am frightened, frightened to death. If someone attacks you in the street or in your home you phone the police, but if it is the police who are attacking you — who do you phone?'

I have written at length about the riots in Brampton and what a devastating effect they had on me. But after that particular harrowing morning Don and I decided that our children would not witness any more chases or violence of any kind. We arranged for my parents to look after them. They lived in a mixed community and were quite a distance from any mine, so had not seen the scenes we had. Packing their cases for them and watching them walk up the street with Don, made me feel so angry. I wanted to run to the riot vans where the police officers were sitting so arrogantly, and yell at them to go away and leave us all alone. After the children left the atmosphere became more and more tense. Anyone going about their own business would find themselves being watched by the officers sitting around in the vans. People became more and more upset, then a rumour started circulating that the police were to impose a curfew on the village. This just added to the problem and people would gather in small groups discussing the situation. The anger seemed to be reaching gigantic proportions, so much so that the air seemed to be full of hostility.

The police must have realised just how bad the situation was becoming and began visiting the local shops to say that they had no intention of imposing anything like that and would people just calm down and go home. This did, however, ease the situation, and the atmosphere became calmer, although there was still a sort of rumbling going on just under the surface and it wouldn't have taken much to ignite the whole situation again.

I became absolutely terrified of these police officers. If any of them passed in a van, or on a bike, I would feel threatened by them, and if ever the Metropolitan Police were known to be in the area, the atmosphere would instantly become hostile. Those policemen were notorious for using unnecessary violence against people, and had become known as the 'Gestapo' of the police force. Like the original group of that name, they seemed to enjoy their work immensely.

During the days of the riots the police began to stop the buses from running through Brampton. They would board the buses at the Yorkshire Traction bus depot and tell everyone who wanted to go into the village to get off and walk. This included the old and young alike.

Sue, my neighbour, came into our house one day, shaking and upset by one such incident. She had been on her way home after doing some shopping, to be home in time to collect her young son from school. She, like the rest, was told to walk. She told them she would be late if she were to meet her son, but it didn't make any difference, she still had to get off. She was so worried, not knowing what Andrew would do if he left school to find no mummy. Would he wait? Or would he try to cross the road to make his own way home? Luckily he was late out of school himself, and was standing looking out of the gate for her when she arrived breathless with running and carrying the shopping bags.

We just couldn't believe that police officers could be so dense — aren't there any fathers in the police force any more? And what would they have done if their wives had been prevented from collecting their children from school on time?

After sleepless nights caused by the rioting, the village became quieter; it was nice to go to bed for some undisturbed sleep.

But every time I fell asleep I would have violent nightmares about the police chasing me through gardens. It would always be the same, I would be running and running with nowhere to hide, then I would wake up, absolutely terrified, at the point where I was grabbed by the hair, from behind, with lots of other police officers crowding round me. This went on for a week or more. I was worn out by working and not daring to go to sleep. I began to dread the nightmares. They were so real and I just didn't want to go to sleep in case I was back in the gardens again.

I had read somewhere that to conquer your fears you had to first face up to whatever it is that frightens you. So I decided to 'face up' to the police by walking through a police line. I had to stop those wretched nightmares somehow. Of course thinking and putting into practice those same thoughts are quite, quite different. Reaching the top of Dearne Road and looking down to where the Alamo was, with the double police line and what seemed like thousands of pickets (probably less than a hundred in reality), I confess I would have liked to turn round and go back home, back to my own four walls. Don asked me if I had changed my mind, and if I was still determined to go through with it. I could quite easily walk up to my parents along the alternative road leading out of Brampton.

He walked with me, up to the last few yards before the police line. He was staying as part of the picket. It was the hardest thing in the world to do, actually to walk up and ask to be excused. I was expecting at any moment to be grabbed, I suppose as in the dream. It all seemed to happen in a haze, the next thing I remember is walking past the riot vans full of more police officers. They were there as back-up, in case of trouble breaking out.

I turned to wave to Don to let him know I was all right. He gave me the thumbs-up sign and waved. I asked him later if I looked as terrified as I felt, and he said that apart from being white I had looked quite normal.

Looking back, I can laugh about it, time heals, but I was glad at the time that no one could see the 'real me' who was a quaking wreck inside. It did stop the nightmares; I only had them occasionally after that, if anything happened to trigger them off again.

CHAPTER ELEVEN

Bitter Winter
'You've done it this time'

The month of November 1984 is jam-packed with memories for me. So many different things happened in my life. Both Don and I realised that the strike was most certainly going to go into Christmas and into the foreseeable future. Both children by this time were desperate for clothes. Both had grown such a lot during the eight months. Darren has always needed new trousers very frequently because he always manages to go through the material at the knee — I'm sure he has razor blades instead of kneecaps — and by this time all but one pair had gone through. So we made the decision to try to earn some money somehow.

The people who owned the cafe were looking for someone to do some handyman-type jobs. My boss, John, was extremely good in business but absolutely useless at repairing, or any DIY jobs, including gardening or decorating, so I was asked if Don would be willing to lend a hand. Over a period of a couple of weeks Don dug and tidied their garden, decorated the bedroom of one of their daughters, and also decorated an extremely large lounge. He also did a few jobs around the cafe itself. Paula, John's wife, was, as I have said before, smashing, and she paid him various amounts: £20 for gardening, £30 for the bedroom and £50 for the lounge, and other amounts for various other jobs. She said she was glad to have found someone so trustworthy and had also got the jobs done at a reasonable price, instead of having to pay professional fees which would have been very costly. She was happy and obviously we were too. We managed at least to buy some of the necessary clothing for the children.

I worked hard at my job and if anyone was absent for any reason, I was only too glad to cover for them, but those times were very rare. How could I earn more money? Jobs were even harder to find because a lot of miners' wives had gone out to fill any jobs which were vacant, even working behind bars, which wouldn't have been heard of before the strike. I racked my brain for days, then I hit on the idea of trying to make some pretty soap pomanders. I had purchased one two years before at a garden fete. A small one had cost £2.50 and after buying the materials they must have made a profit. So I sat there and took mine to bits to find out how the complicated ribbon-work was done. It took over an hour, but, yes, I could make them as well. The thing was I needed funds to buy the soap, straight pins, paper ribbon and artificial flowers for the trim. So I had to ask Don again to lend me his fire station money. I had to convince him first that I could actually make them that well. I made one and sold it within an hour to our milkman, for his wife. I charged £1.45 for one made out of a large size block of soap with plain ribbon, with open daisy flowers for trim. I also began to make prettier ones out of the same size soap but made with a pretty lace ribbon instead of plain, and finished this kind off with either rosebud trim or roses — they could choose. These I sold for £1.60, and I was more than happy with the 60p profit I made on each one.

I was astonished at the demand for them. I suppose with them being at a reasonable price people could still buy a little something for Christmas. Children also came to ask me to make them for their mummies for Christmas. I had such a demand that I would still be up in the early hours of the morning trying to fill orders. I didn't want to let anyone down, least of all the children. In the end I taught Don to pin the soaps for me so I would only have to 'dress' them and put the final touches to them. Over the weeks leading up to Christmas I made between 250 and 300 pomanders. Christmas Eve was a relief to my sore and blistered fingers, but to be able to buy gifts for our children was well worth the effort. I've never made one from that day to this, because I became sick of the sight and smell of them in the end.

The lead-up to Christmas also included helping Tilly and Les to raise funds for two large Christmas parties for the miners' children. The first party for up to eight-year-olds and the second for the eight to sixteen-year-olds.

I didn't do a great deal really, I organised a couple of pie and pea evenings again, but most of the funds came from holding auctions. I went to a cash-and-carry a couple of times to buy paper plates, but little more. One of the reasons for this was that my health had started to deteriorate. I caught a cold and this seemed to linger on to another, then I began to have asthma attacks during one particularly heavy cold. I had had attacks some years before, but these were found to be brought on by aerosol sprays. Since then I had avoided them and used alternatives such as stick deodorants and 'squirty' polish instead of sprays — I had been fine since then.

I began to have other infections and became listless. Don noticed that I seemed to go into asthma attacks whenever anyone smoked in my presence. Although he smoked five or six a day he had to go either outside or into another room when I was at home. But I couldn't avoid going into public places where smokers were. For example, travelling on buses to get to work became a nightmare.

The group organising the party also had people who liked to smoke. Many of them sympathised and avoided smoking in my presence. One particular lady, however, objected to everyone making allowances just for one person — I can't really blame her, but after two extremely bad attacks brought on by the said woman sitting close to me at meetings, I had to stop attending and had to rely on people who did go to relay what had been decided upon.

I elected to make all the Christmas table decorations as well as the novelty cakes for the 'tinies' party. One large cake was to be donated by a catering firm Les and Tilly had dealings with in their business. I had agreed to make them because I had made a few for my own children's birthday parties. I didn't profess to be really good but it would have cost a fortune to have them made professionally.

I started to make them on my day off at seven o'clock in the morning, and finally fell into bed at two o'clock the following morning. In that time I had made four basin snowmen, decorated with hats, buttons and faces; also eight parcels, all different colours with the piped on address of the parish hall where we were to have the party. I then made a special 'house' cake. The roof was made of dairy chocolate buttons with icing poured on to look like snow. The door and windows were made out of sweets — the windows, for example, were four Spangle sweets to make coloured panes. The fence was made out of peppermint Matchmakers.

I also made three large cakes, two were traditional snow scenes and the other was like one I had seen in a cook book. The large square was divided into smaller ones by piping and silver cashews and small pieces of plastic holly were dotted in alternate squares. This one and the two others were for the older children's party. The pleasure these cakes gave to the children and adults alike was worth all the hard work which went into them. However, the icing bag had hardly been put away when there was knocking at the door the next evening.

'Jackie, please help, there's been an accident to the donated cake which was delivered this afternoon,' said Sue Hickling, one of the group organisers. I went with her to the house to see just what had happened. Sue, trying to stop dust landing on the cake or any damage happening, had covered it with a table cloth. On removing it to show the cake to visitors she found that the piping hadn't set properly and the cloth had severely damaged the intricate icing detail. It was quite bad and I didn't really see what could be done. Everyone in the room seemed to be looking at me to 'do something'. Well, if I could it would have to be in my own home because the few icing things I had were there, plus I would not have been able to work in a strange place.

What a sight it was seeing Don and Sue's husband, Gordon, stagger through the streets carrying the cake. The cake was three feet by two feet, and quite heavy as well as cumbersome. Every time they went up and down the kerbs I thought it would smash to bits. It would have been funny if it hadn't been serious. It wasn't until the cake was sitting on the table in the dining room that it really hit me. I had to somehow repair that mess! After Don saw Gordon to the door he came to stand behind me to view the cake.

'Well, Mrs Keating, you've done it this time!' he said. He didn't have to say a word. What on earth would I do with it? I must be the world's best at getting myself into situations which I could avoid if only I could learn to say 'No, I'm sorry.' Well it was no good crying over spilt milk, I had to at least try. The first problem was to remove all the damaged icing without damaging even more. The transport of the cake hadn't caused any more damage, just scattered the debris around the cake making it lodge between the writing and the other features of the cake. Whoever made it had gone to an awful lot of trouble and must have spent hours making it!

I eventually solved the problem of clearing up the mess by using a clean dry pastry brush and 'sweeping' the mess away onto greaseproof paper. The piping had been done on the pure white cake with brilliant crimson icing, and that was a problem in itself. Most dyes are post-box red. I walked miles the next day, trying all over Wombwell to find a match. I found one eventually, in Les's shop, having tramped for miles. But it still wasn't near enough — when I piped some damaged wording, it showed up quite badly against the old. So the only thing left to do was to re-ice the entire area which had been done in crimson. I managed to scrape away the old lettering with a sharp knife but I was terribly aware that if I made a mess now, it would be permanent. Crimson is hardly the colour to play around with. Somewhere around 2.30 a.m. I fell into bed. Don, Gordon and Sue were delighted with the results, but I wouldn't say I was because I could see all the wobbly bits where my hands had been shaking. Don said I was a 'worry wart' and that no one else would notice. He was right, by the way, no one did!

The relief was astronomical as I had been so afraid of letting the others down. I also found a sort of pleasure out of knowing I seemed to have a hidden talent, either that or I did it out of pure desperation.

Unfortunately I was due to work on the day of the party. I asked a work mate if she would mind working the day of the party in my place, and in return I would work the afternoon of Christmas Eve. She agreed wholeheartedly to the straight swap of shifts.

The following day, however, my so-called friend said that I still owed her a favour. On asking her what she wanted, she replied by saying she wanted me to work New Year's Eve afternoon for her. She would fill in for me any shift after that. I had no alternative but to agree to this. I found out later that this 'friend' had managed to arrange for herself two whole weeks off work during the Christmas period. While I would only have Christmas Day and Boxing Day off. But that's life.

Don was absolutely furious, which led to an argument between us. I was putting the party before the family, I could have spent more time at home if I hadn't made stupid agreements because of a party.

In the end I had to agree to change the arrangement back

again. I didn't like doing this and was unhappy about going back on my word. But I was even more unhappy about being accused of not thinking about my family first, because nothing and no one has ever been put before them, ever.

I did realise the 'friend' was taking unfair advantage. This was one of Don's grievances during the argument — that I had let her get away with it. I still didn't think this a good enough reason to go back on my word, though I knew Don had my own interests at heart, and I do manage to get myself into these predicaments quite regularly, so I suppose he meant well by insisting that I 'do something about it' this time. It doesn't matter how much I try I just can't seem to change and I freely admit it has brought me quite a bit of grief in the past, and it probably will in the future too.

The party had also been the reason for my total and absolute loss of temper. It was concerning a family who had helped out a lot at all the pie and pea evenings by running around fetching and carrying, and had used a great deal of petrol, but wouldn't think of charging a penny, even though things were as hard for them as they were for everyone else.

The group I was helping had a meeting to decide who could come to the parties and where the limits were. The area they decided on exempted the Eccles family. The group asked me if I would explain the situation to them, that their two little girls couldn't come because of the boundary they had drawn up. I argued that these two little girls had worked their hearts out to help 'mummy and me' make money, so they could go to the party we were working for. How would two little girls understand about 'boundaries' and that they couldn't go after all? I was beside myself with fury. If I hadn't left the room I'm sure I would have struck someone. They weren't going to tell the family themselves, they wanted me to do the dirty work for them. I told them in no uncertain terms that they could stuff it, and that I would never help any of them again if they could use people like that, only to dispense with them when the hard work had been done and not allow them a share in the 'fun' time.

Tilly found out about how upset I was and rang to find out why. In all the time she had known me she had never seen me so angry and upset. I told her exactly how I felt and how I would never be part of a group which could treat children so badly. Tilly said she would talk to some of the group involved and ring back later. She hit on the idea that the parents of the children should be invited as special guests, to judge the fancy dress with Richard, and of course the children had to come along because they couldn't stay at home alone, could they? I realised then, and do now, that some kind of limit had to be made, but I also believe that the people who make these hard and fast rules can also break them again, in very special circumstances. If I hadn't intervened, those two little girls would have had their hearts broken with disappointment. I knew how much they had looked forward to going to the party, because they had talked of little else for weeks.

One of the nicest parts of the small ones' party was that everyone 'dressed up' in fancy dress. There were rag dolls, Andy Pandy, a large baby, many more. I wore an old-fashioned swimming costume with knee-length leggings and mop hat. We also ran a fancy dress competition for the little ones and I had written to Richard Wells to ask him if he would judge it for us. Unfortunately he was working, but he managed to come anyway, with Ian and Brian, to televise the party. Richard judged the little ones, before the children went off to watch Punch and Judy. The highlight of the day was when the children watched themselves on television, which caused great excitement. The other helpers having had all their hard work televised also found great pleasure in Richard and crew coming back to Brampton. So I guess the bridges were becoming a little stronger without them even realising it.

I would have liked things not to have been quite so hectic

because I, by now, looked upon Richard as more of a friend than a 'media person', and we very rarely found time to have a chat. The time he had found to come to see everyone in Brampton more than compensated for that.

The older children's disco went equally well, but my memories are with the 'tinies' and their party. The squelchy jellies, the laughter and finally the visit to see Santa Claus. Nothing is quite the same as the 'magic' the very little ones have when sitting on Santa's knee, and yes, it was worth every minute. I even managed to convince myself of that when staggering home, totally shattered, at one o'clock in the morning, after cleaning up cakes with the tops half bitten off, and sticky fingerprints. I would still like to know who managed to get that cream cake to stick on the wall half way up to the ceiling. A future marksman to be sure!

Christmas itself was smashing, everyone around us was determined to enjoy themselves come what may. So the atmosphere was warm and very gay.

Mum, Dad, Alan, my youngest brother, and my family were invited to go to a party at Garry's house. We set off in high spirits, singing carols and telling jokes in turn. As we approached Garry's house the strike was brought back forcefully into our minds. Sitting outside his gate was a riot van — full of police officers. They watched us closely as we walked past them and in through the gate. It's quite an unnerving experience being watched like that, as if you're up to something even though you're not doing anything wrong.

When we entered Garry's house he told us the police had arrived a couple of hours earlier. His neighbour, a miner, had gone back to work and had been back quite some time. Some of his workmates had found out and the police had come to move him, lock, stock and barrel with a removal van, to prevent any verbal or physical attack on his family or home from other miners still on strike. They had just finished boarding up the windows and doors when we arrived, hence the riot van.

The evening was very pleasant, good food, drink and games played with all three children. Because of the cigarette smoke I would occasionally leave the room for a while. I went up to one of Garry's bedrooms to see if the police had gone. No, they were still sitting there; the street was deserted and quiet, I don't know what they were expecting but whatever it was, it didn't materialise.

Looking down at the police van sitting there, I began to remember my childhood days when police officers were part of the community. One council house in the road where I lived always had an officer and his family living there. His wife and children would pop in like any other neighbour. One such family was called Howlands. They had three boys, the oldest David, was older than me by a couple of weeks, then there was Christopher, then baby Clifford named after his father.

I was perhaps five or six years old at the time, when David asked if he could be my 'boyfriend' and we should run away together; we 'ran' as far as his back garden to his 'den'. But unfortunately, the jam sandwiches and packet of sweets which his mum had given him ran out, so he decided that he would 'run away' some other time and went home for his tea instead — talk about fickle. That was how life was then, we would run in and out of each other's houses like children do. His dad, I remember, went out to work like my dad did, but was a policeman instead of a miner. All the children would watch for him coming home from work with his uniform on and a cape around his shoulders. He was known as David's dad and would be greeted by all the children on his way home. If ever there was a problem people would go to 'have a little word' with PC Howland. Even the children would go to him. I remember once finding a badly injured cat — two dogs had savaged it. I ran as fast as I could to fetch David's dad because he would know what to do. Of course he came, holding my hand, to 'see' and took the poor little thing to his home. I remember it died soon afterwards. But the memory was there, that policemen were 'trusted' people. How times change!

My memory of the police had always been that 'they were dads too'. Looking out at the riot van brought it home to me, those days were gone, never to return. When I was a child any police officers in the area on duty wouldn't have been sitting there, they would have been invited to come inside — my father would have been one of the first. They would have been offered the warmest seat in the house in front of the roaring fire, then plied with mince pies, scones and a hot steaming mug of tea, in a word 'welcomed'. Instead now my parents had developed a deep hatred. Don despises them because they use the law when and if they feel like it. Nikki and I are frightened of them and Darren loathes them like no child should.

Why has society changed so much? So many good things have happened to improve the value of life, yet at the same time, people have somehow become devalued in the quest for possessions, wealth, fame and ambition to 'get to the top,' leaving the poor, sick and vulnerable ones behind.

I wonder how many people would give anything to have the old-fashioned beat bobby living amongst them now, instead of police running around in cars so distant and remote that the elderly don't feel safe any more and spend most of their lives behind bolted and chained doors. Yes, the police have moved with the 'times' with their computers, Hooley vans etc., but has it been for the better? I seriously doubt that.

I went back downstairs and joined in the fun but somehow the sadness I felt stayed with me for the rest of the evening and still returns at any quiet moment.

It was hard to return to normality after Christmas. I suppose everyone feels a little 'down', quite naturally, after the big build up leading to Christmas Day, but somehow the days seemed bleaker, longer and bitterly cold. I always feel the cold during winter months, but that winter I felt almost numb. Don went coke-picking every day without fail, but it wasn't enough to keep a fire in the grate, so we resorted to fetching the paraffin stove in from the shed where it had been thrown some years before. The stove was a double barrel burner, but as soon as the children left for school we had to turn one burner off and the other one down as far as it would go to save on fuel. The trouble was, the fumes from the stove also brought on my asthma attacks. We ventilated the room by opening the window, but that defeated the object of warming up the room, so it all became a vicious circle.

The atmosphere also changed at work. Before Christmas Paula and John, the owners of the cafe, and the workers, had been mostly all right about it, only discussing the violence from time to time. Now the strike never seemed to be out of the conversation. I would hear customers and staff airing their views and I would only on occasions become involved because I was only too aware that to get into any kind of argument with the customers would result in my losing my job.

Walking into work one day and changing in the office, I became aware that John and a fellow worker were once again discussing the strike. They were so intent on exchanging views that they didn't notice me actually walk behind them to go into the corner of the room, to where I occasionally wash up.

John was saying quite venomously that he hoped that every miner would lose their job and he hoped that they would end up spending all their lives on the dole. The fellow worker went on to say that miners and their families were nothing but yobs and thugs, and hoped that the ones caught by the policemen would be sent to prison for a long time.

I was totally devastated. So this was how they really thought of me and my family. Dear God, how that hurt! I've always worked hard, always doing everything asked of me, and sometimes more. I don't know how I got through that day — I felt raw inside. I just wanted to go away from these people and never have to work with them again. The reality was of course that I had to keep working to feed my family. If I handed in my notice I would have to wait six weeks to be able to claim anything on their behalf. It hurt so much, to know that they actually hoped that we as a family would be thrown on the dole and Don sent to prison. Something died inside me during those few minutes, but I made the decision that when the strike was finally over I would never work there again. My trust in them had gone. I would never know if what they were saying was the truth or a complete sham. What did they really think about me? Did they really think of Don, the man who had had the freedom of their home, as a yob or a thug?

To be fair, they had been good to me up to then. Paula occasionally would send me home with half a pie for the children. During the Christmas period we had also been invited to her home to a party, where we all had a smashing time.

A bitter argument went on in my head. One part of me would say, 'Don't be silly, they are just letting off steam, think about the many times they've been good to you and the family.' The other part of me would argue back again, 'That was before I found out how they really thought about us as a mining family.' The see-sawing kept up all that day and into the following weeks. In the end I began to dread going to work. I would sit on the bus praying to myself and saying, 'Try to get through today without making a fool of yourself by breaking down, or saying anything you would only regret.' This trauma inside eventually took its toll and I began to have terrible pains in my stomach. When I went to bed I wouldn't be able to sleep because the pain would be so intense. I would have to get up again and spend many hours pacing the floor between the kitchen and the lounge. Also, certain foods would bring the pain on, sometimes more severely. These would be any fried foods, vinegar, coffee and any citrus fruits. I know I should have gone to the doctor sooner, but prescriptions cost money, and money was so tight that I felt it to be an added burden on our finances. You're probably thinking I could get free prescriptions, but I couldn't because I was not claiming supplementary benefit and these came into that category. We had tried at one particular time, when we were so financially desperate, to see if we were entitled to Family Income Supplement, with Don working so many hours for the Fire Service. But we were turned down, even when we appealed. The silly thing was, a miner's wife who worked in the canteen of the fire station did receive FIS, but Don, who worked as a fireman, couldn't. We never could figure out the logic in that. We just assume that someone at the 'top' brought in a few more rules for miners, the reason being, anyone working as a retained fireman could be on the dole and any earnings from the fire station were exempted because firemen come under a special category. Now suddenly they weren't so special any more.

I eventually went to the doctors. Don threatened to drag me there physically if I didn't go under my own steam. I had managed to avoid worrying Don about the pains for a number of weeks. I just let him assume the pain was a menstrual pain which was usual for me. Obviously, living in close proximity with someone, your partner soon realises something isn't quite right, and in a short space of time too.

The doctor diagnosed a suspected stomach ulcer, and the medication she gave me was worth every penny of the prescription. I also had to eat small meals at regular intervals and avoid the things which triggered the attacks. Could I also learn not to worry so much, and learn to relax more — a lot easier to say than do.

CHAPTER TWELVE

Back to Work

'We're going back to work but for how long?'

On the afternoon of 2 March 1985, a newsflash appeared on television — 'The Miners' Strike is Over'.

I was sitting at my sewing machine, trying to repair some of the children's clothing when the announcement came over on Nikki's portable television. Don had also seen it on the television in the lounge. We met at the kitchen door — there was no excitement, no euphoria because at long last it was all over. Nothing, only deep, deep sadness. All the hardships, heartache and suffering had been for nothing. There was no doubt about it, many, many jobs would go now. We had all given it our best shot, sacrificed so many things to try to save jobs, but it still hadn't been enough. Don said, 'Well, love, this is it, we're going back to work but for how long?'

The next day, after a meeting, it was decided that the men from Cortonwood would return to work, not defeated but with their heads held high, behind the banner. The following morning the entire village turned out to watch our men march back into work. People shouted to them to hold their heads up and that no one could have asked any more of these men than what they had given in their desperate fight to save their jobs and their communities.

The elderly and the women alike had tears in their eyes, watching the men march down the main street. We were so proud of them in their march, showing so much dignity and courage, facing the media.

On reaching the Alamo, however, they found that some Kent miners were blocking the entrance to the pit lane. They had now taken over the picket hut and they were picketing the Cortonwood miners out!

The entire procession ground to a halt — total confusion ensued. No one knew what was going on. The NUM leadership had ordered that the men should return to work but the men couldn't obey the order because it would mean breaking the one golden rule of all the trade unions: no one should cross a picket line.

Eventually everyone began moving off, back up the main street, to wait outside the Miners Welfare, where the NUM officials were trying to make some sense of it all in the strike centre. After about an hour, one of the officials came out to stand on the wall and asked everyone to go home for now until something was sorted out. Don and I decided to go to visit my parents to see how Dad had fared at his mine. Apparently the Kent miners had put pickets on most of the surrounding pits, so where did that leave our miners?

Walking back from Wombwell we passed the Kent miners sitting in their transit van. They looked totally and utterly fed up. Don went across the road to speak to them through the open window. They hadn't received much hospitality from the local people since they had been there and said that quite a few people were acting quite bitterly towards them. I could understand that, because it had been difficult to return to work anyway, knowing the fight had been lost, but they had robbed our men of returning to work with dignity and that was the essence of the situation. Don invited them to come to our home for a shower and a meal, they were quite welcome to what little we had.

Around seven o'clock that evening, two of the Kent miners knocked on the door to accept our hospitality. After the initial meeting when we introduced ourselves, we went about making these strangers welcome by making a cup of tea and a meal, while they took it in turn to use the bathroom.

Afterwards, we all sat down for a chat. They told us the reason why they had put a picket on Cortonwood. Many Kent miners had been sacked during the strike and they were picketing to stop the return to work without an agreement being reached first on these men being reinstated. We parted company that night on quite amicable terms, and with perhaps a little more understanding of their positions.

The next morning there was a meeting at the Parish Hall, where it was all thrashed out. Don went to the rostrum to plead with his colleagues to at least give the Kent miners a fair hearing, but to no avail. Eventually it was decided that the men should go back to work and that the Kent miners should withdraw.

Unfortunately they didn't give the officials time to contact the miners who were left at the picket hut, so the television that night showed scenes of the men from Cortonwood marching through a picket line of Kent miners, and a final shot of one of the miners' placards lying forlornly on the ground after being trampled underfoot.

The media also came to visit us again. Triona did a final interview for BBC Radio. Richard didn't come; however, he did a really wonderful piece on a village near Barnsley. Someone from the national news contacted him and he passed on our phone number to Mike McKay, a BBC news correspondent from London. He visited us with a television crew. I found him to be a tremendously nice person and in the short time he was there we discussed many things, including his own family.

The interview went very well, and I for once was quite at ease in their company. The recording, however, didn't go out on the news. During our interview we had been asked what was the very first thing we would buy. This was a standing joke between Don and myself, for during the year-long strike almost every beaker and cup in the house had been broken, and we had promised ourselves 'they' would be the first thing we purchased. Don said he was sick of drinking out of jam jars — he fibs well, it wasn't quite that bad, but nearly. The interview depicted us, at least in our eyes, as an ordinary family, filled with a little sadness and yet at the same time still able to laugh about our predicament.

The footage that was televised was revolting. It showed a nasty scene, and then one individual spitting on to the camera lens. I found the whole thing to be very distasteful — who on earth wanted to see spit running down the television screen? Mike phoned us later to say that there hadn't been enough time in the slot for our interview. I was glad he rang, it showed that he hadn't just done a story piece and then forgotten about us.

But from that day to this I've wanted to know who chooses between all the stories to be televised, and why did that horrible piece have to be shown, unless it was used to show the country that all miners and their families are nothing but morons and have disgusting habits into the bargain.

CHAPTER THIRTEEN

Suspended
'I hurt inside, oh how I hurt'

On Tuesday, 5 March 1985, Don walked down the pit lane along with the other men. I had been with him during the second march back, not actually in the march, but I walked down on the pavement beside them.

I told him I wouldn't go down into the pit yard with him, I would sooner wait for him opposite the Alamo. I stood chatting to two old ex-colliers and time seemed to pass pleasantly enough. After about an hour I realised that most of the men who had walked down had already returned. Where was Don? After more time had passed I stopped one of the men I knew from the village, to ask if he had seen Don, if he knew where he was.

'I'm sorry love, I think he's one of the men who has been suspended. He's in with the manager right now. Go home and wait for him there.' I couldn't believe it, no this couldn't happen to us! He hadn't done anything. He really hadn't done anything wrong, only called a police inspector some name when he had used violence on him, and I couldn't blame him for that.

I didn't listen to the man, I didn't want to go home. My place was to be here for Don. He would need me now more than at any time in our marriage. I stood there so long that everyone else drifted away leaving me alone.

I must have been the only one in the village to watch the Alamo being dismantled bit by bit until finally a large earth-moving machine came and scooped up all that was remaining, including the still smouldering stove, along with the memories that went with it.

After an eternity, one of the men, a miner and a retained fireman, walked up the lane and stopped to speak to me. 'Have you heard? Don's been sacked.' I don't know how I kept standing. It was like a blow to my whole body. The voice in my head kept saying, 'No, this can't be right, there's been a mistake, there's got to have been a mistake!'

I went home because I couldn't trust myself not to show Don up by breaking down and making a fool of myself in public. That walk home was the longest and hardest of my entire life. People would stop to speak and I couldn't answer them. There seemed to be a huge ball inside my throat and chest. I'll never know what people must have thought of me that day, I must have seemed so ignorant and rude.

On reaching home I found my way into the living room — I just couldn't take another step — and sank down to the floor with my head resting on my arms on one of the chairs. I began to cry, very quietly at first, until huge sobs took over. I couldn't believe that they could be so callous. Dear God, hadn't we suffered enough? What about all those times they had phoned Don out when there was an emergency at the pit, he had never let them down, be it weekend or during the night he had always been there. Why Don? Why?

Then the pain started. I had lower abdominal pain, stomach pain, and most of all the pain from somewhere deep inside. I needed someone, where was someone? Anyone. Didn't they realise I needed someone sometimes too? I needed someone to support me, to jolly me along, the way I had done with my friends, neighbours and family. Please help me someone! No one came. No one. The sobs seemed to take over, they were so bad that I found it difficult to breathe and went into a very bad asthma attack. I managed to crawl over to where my work bag was, to use my Ventolin inhaler. However with not much effect, as I was crying so hard. The pain in my stomach was excruciating but there was no way I could have made it into the kitchen where I kept my medication.

I seemed to be in my own private hell for hours, but it was perhaps only half an hour later when there came a knock at the door. Sue, my neighbour, came into the room looking for me. 'Jackie, whatever's wrong, what's happened? Stop it! You're making yourself ill. Tell me. This isn't like you, please stop.'

A voice in my head yelled back, 'Don't you see, this is me . . . I hurt too . . . I'm not really a tower of strength. Doesn't anyone else realise what it costs me to pin a smile on my face and to be always the one to offer a shoulder to cry on. I hurt inside, oh how I hurt!'

I still hadn't managed to make any sense to Sue when Don came home a few minutes later. He was more than concerned because I couldn't control the sobs — it really wasn't like me. Before the strike I was a very private person and if ever I cried I always made sure no one was around to witness it. Plus Don is like all of the male species, he hates to see a woman cry because it makes him feel so inadequate, not knowing whether to give comfort or take off and leave them to it.

Very soon afterwards Sue left to fetch Andrew from school. I realised my own children would be home soon. I had to pull myself together. I got up off the floor, sat bolt upright in one of the chairs and kept telling myself over and over again to stop it! I tried so very hard but the tears just wouldn't stop. One of the things going round in my head was that I had to go to work tomorrow, then the next day and the next. No! I didn't want to go, I didn't want to overhear them saying 'Serves him right.' It was already so hard to walk up to the bus stop to board a bus taking me to a place I really didn't want to go. Two people seemed to be in a bitter argument within my head. The first was saying, 'Stop it! Stop being stupid! Don needs you more than ever and you're not helping him, being like this. Stop . .

Stop!' The other part of me seemed to yell, 'I don't want to stop, I can't stop — I'm falling to pieces and I'm not "strong" any more. Can't anyone see that?'

Don brought my medication to at least stop the stomach pain, then went to make me a cup of tea. He sat beside me holding my hand.

'Listen love, tomorrow you're going to hand in your notice. You can't go on like this any more. You're making yourself so ill.' Between sobs I tried to argue that we would need the money even more now. All the people we owed money to, like the mortgage and rates people, would all be wanting their money. Who would feed our children? He held me in his arms, saying we would manage somehow; we had up to now, hadn't we?

I knew deep down he was right — I was a total physical and emotional wreck, so tired, so very worn out.

Much later that day, Don told me what had happened. On going into work to have his checks released (checks are discs which are used to know who is down the mine; the miner keeps one and the other is left at the pit top).

Don had been asked if he would go to the interview room to see the pit manager. On entering the room he found the manager, and a man taking notes, there was Dougie Robertson, Roy Hart (representing the NUM) and two other men. Don and the two other men were given letters and told in no uncertain terms that they were to be suspended indefinitely. Mr Hartley, the pit manager, said that none of this was anything to do with him, he was just following orders from the Headquarters at area.

Dougie tried to intervene on behalf of the men but to no avail. Don during this time thought this to be 'rich'. Dougie had been arrested before him and his trial was still pending along with Don's, so who had decided to suspend some and not others? All three men were asked if they had any comment to make, but on seeing the man scribbling away, Don decided against making any comment. It would have been unprintable in any case!

On leaving the office Don opened the letter, to read the following:

> Dear Mr Keating,
>
> In view of the serious charges pending against you, and the circumstances surrounding those charges, you are suspended from work with the National Coal Board until further notice.
>
> I shall be investigating this matter in due course. After the completion of my investigation, a decision will be made as to any disciplinary proceedings which may be appropriate against you, including whether you should be dismissed from the Board's employment.
>
> Yours sincerely,
> A Hartley
> Colliery Manager.

I asked Don later how he had felt during that time. He said he was at first stunned, then angry, but it wasn't until he was walking down the pit lane home again that the reality of it struck him. He had racked his brains trying to think of an easy way to tell me and the children. What he hadn't thought of was the grapevine telling me first, and especially exaggerating the rumour, and making it much worse by saying he had actually been sacked.

Entering the house and seeing me in such a state was Don's worst moment of the entire strike. In all of that time 'Jackie' had been the tough one, taking and resolving one problem after another. He said he felt that if 'Jackie' was all right the rest of the family would be, because she would make sure they were.

He hadn't known whether to 'phone a doctor, but thought it would probably upset me even more. (He was right not to, it would have.) He had realised over the past couple of weeks the effect that working at the cafe was having on me (there I was thinking I had hidden it quite well). I would become withdrawn and sort of 'went into a shell' (Don's expression) whenever it was time to leave for work. He said I would only be something like my normal self when I had finished on Friday evening until Tuesdays came round, then I looked like I was being haunted and barely had a word to say to anyone.

It wasn't until that morning, when he actually made me talk about it, that he realised it was 'that bad' for me to keep going. We, or, should I say, he, decided that as soon as he had his first pay packet I would finish work. My health came before money. Besides, we had managed on so little, that his wage would seem like a fortune in comparison.

One of the things which had worried me so much about Don's suspension had been money, to keep my family. I'm very ashamed to say that I doubted the men of Cortonwood and the people of Brampton.

I had thought to myself 'Why should anyone give even a little amount each week to help the Keating family?' They themselves had endured one whole year of hardship so why should they help us. Don was after all one of the thugs and yobs of society. This was our problem, not theirs. I didn't believe that once they were back at work they would even have the time of day for us. Who could we turn to? My family? Yes, they would help but they had so little themselves, we couldn't ask them to give us any of the money they were about to start having again, now Dad was back at work.

Would Don's family help? There was no way either Don or I would ever ask (they didn't offer either). Don told me that he had been told that the men from Cortonwood would 'look after us'. I felt I needed a safety net. What if they didn't help us? Who would feed Nikki and Darren?

We went to the DHSS to find out if we could be helped. We felt so degraded sitting in that bare room waiting our turn. We were aware that the people who had been waiting before us were interviewed at a 'window', and their conversation could be heard by most of the people in the room.

Eventually it was our turn. After explaining about Don being suspended we were told 'sorry, we can't help. People like you are to be classed as being on strike.' We knew Don wasn't on strike — she knew he wasn't, but the instructions had come from 'Head Office'. Don't the people on high like their pound of flesh!

So Don and I had to wait. On Friday of that week someone telephoned to ask Don if he would mind popping down to see someone at the pit. He was given a pay packet with some money donated from other men's pockets. I can't put into words how we felt about that — if I live to be a hundred, I will never forget. We were also given food parcels for two weeks. I suppose they knew us only too well, and realised that we would never have gone to collect them ourselves.

The following day I had to literally drag myself to work. I felt and looked terrible and had barely slept. I handed in my notice, but somehow didn't get any relief out of it.

That was on Thursday, and I had Friday, then Wednesday to Friday the following week to work. Don urged me to go and see the doctor and to serve my notice 'on the sick'. I refused, one reason was that to finish like that went against the grain, and also it would have left them in a mess, trying to find someone to cover for me. I felt I had to finish my employment with them in a decent manner — that was only fair. I must admit I regretted my stubbornness on many, many occasions during my final three days. I finished my time at the cafe as I had started, washing up. This was a very demanding job at the best of times. The dishwasher had packed up months before and hadn't been replaced, so every plate, dish and pan was washed by hand, then dried and placed on the relevant shelves. When I was well I was perhaps the only one working there who would manage to keep up, without a massive backlog. But those three days were the hardest and longest of my life (apart from the day of Don's arrest). I just couldn't keep up. Piles and piles of pots and pans surrounded me, every inch was taken up, including the floor around my feet. I would become upset and when I became upset the pain would start up, then the asthma attacks would start. I was in quite a state, and the other members of the staff, Paula and John would have to come to lend a hand, and during the last day I was told to sit down and rest for a while. I really don't know how I got home during that time.

The day before my last working day I was walking down home when I noticed Roy Hart, the NUM President, walking out of his gate. On seeing me he crossed to speak.

'Have you seen Don yet?'

'No I'm just returning home from work. Why?'

'I've just had a phone call from work. The manager wants to see me and the suspended men.'

'What do you think it means, will they be reinstated?' I asked him. Then my stomach did a sort of jump. 'You don't think they're going to sack them?' Roy said, 'I don't think so, just keep your fingers crossed.'

When I entered the house I found a note from Don saying pretty much the same thing Roy had told me. How long that next hour seemed. I paced the floor until the children came home, then, more for something to do other than the eternal walking back and forth between rooms, I made a drink and prepared tea, with my ears trained on the gate, listening for the latch to go and Don's footsteps.

Finally, the wait was over. Don came in and I looked at his face to see if there was anything there to give me a clue to what the news was to be. I wanted to know, but at the same time I was terrified of what he had to tell me. Perhaps Don could see it in my face because he put his arms around me.

'It's all right love, it's all right. I've been reinstated and I start work on Monday.'

The children hearing Dad had come home and hearing the news into the bargain, went berserk. They threw their arms around his neck, shouting 'Yippee!' and making a hell of a fuss.

I had sunk into a chair no longer able to take it in. I suppose, to be truthful, I had half convinced myself that he would be sacked.

Darren said, 'Mum, Dad's got his job back,' then he looked at me and said, 'Dad, is Mum going to get better now?' Don came across to me and took me in his arms and said, 'I hope so, son, I hope so.'

The rest of that day is a blur. Don rang my parents, via their next-door neighbours, to tell them of the news.

Later that night when the children were in bed, he told me that this meeting had been a re-run of the first, but instead of Dougie being there, Roy Hart and Jack Wake had been the NUM representatives.

This time they were given another letter, obviously typed in advance.

> Dear Sir,
> I refer to the discussions we had today. Further to my letter of the 4 March, 1985, I am now in a position to withdraw the suspension imposed on that date. I would, however, warn you that any future action of a similar nature may result in disciplinary procedures being instigated.
> Yours faithfully,
> A Hartley,
> Manager.

Mr Hartley had had a change of heart. He said that he had been the one to suspend Don and the people at the Area had nothing to do with it. He asked all three men if they wished to make any comment. I think Don shocked them all because he told them what he thought. He didn't blame the local management, he suggested that it had been an area manager who had instigated the suspensions and he (Don) would like to go on record as saying he thought them to be callous, barbaric individuals. (Knowing Don, it wasn't said quite like that!) He also went on to say his wife had been made very ill by these people, and he wished them to end up in a place a lot hotter than on earth. He also told them that he hadn't been to trial yet and who did they really think they were? Didn't justice work in our country any more, that they could be the judge and jury and give out sentences at will?

Don returned to work on Monday 18 March 1985, two weeks after the other men of Cortonwood started on the afternoon shift.

After receiving some new boots etc., and going through a short refresher course on using a self-rescuer, he boarded the chair to ride down the shaft for the first time in over a year.

When he disembarked he was greeted by the men on the day shift, waiting in the barriers to ride out of the pit. They all broke out in spontaneous applause (Don said he felt a right wally). Then as he passed by them they took it in turns to shake his hand or pat his back, welcoming him back to work.

When we had moved to Yorkshire from Nottingham and Don had found a job working for the Coal Board, one of the things he had worried about was being accepted by them, so you can imagine how he felt about this reception, and the care and generosity the men had shown him during his suspension.

Unknown to us, Don's solicitor, Gareth Pearce, having heard about his suspension, had started the wheels in motion for a High Court hearing. The law of the country is that you are innocent until proven guilty, and that takes place in a courtroom. One of the things which had annoyed Gareth was that, even though Don had been on conditional bail for months, he had still done vital work in the shafts to keep the mine open for essential safety checks.

He and a group of men had volunteered to do the brake tests on the cages. Without this being done no one, not even the most senior of the management, could ride down into the mine.

Don and the group also did the cappling work. The capple is a piece of equipment which secures the winding rope to the top of the chair, and this has to be changed every three months, by law. If this isn't done the safety checks, to make sure that there isn't excess flooding or a build-up of the highly explosive methane gas, cannot go ahead.

None of the men accepted any wages for the full five days work they did periodically throughout that year. The money was donated to charity on their behalf by the NCB. They did, however, accept £1 a day in payment from the Union. This was eventually paid to Don during the last week of his suspension. Gareth had arranged a High Court hearing to be heard in London on 18 March.

Obviously the NCB would have had to be served notice of the proceedings and given the date to appear in court.

Gareth had tried to phone us during Thursday, 14 March to ask Don to travel down to London to appear in court. She had taken out an injunction to prevent the NCB suspending Don because his court case hadn't been heard yet, so they had jumped the gun. Gareth hadn't got a reply during the afternoon, and by the time she had phoned again Don had been reinstated forty minutes earlier. I'm sure we can be forgiven for concluding that Don's reinstatement was a little more than coincidence?

CHAPTER FOURTEEN

Guilt
'Is it something I've done?'

Before life could once again settle down to something like
normality, we had to first face up to the debts incurred by the
strike, and these seemed insurmountable. Both the children had
grown so much during that year, and the few clothes we had
managed to buy had been worn out by their frequency of washing
and wearing. We needed money for household expenditure too.

Luckily for us we found help in the shape of a financial
adviser, Andrew Charles, who we had met in the process of
buying our home. He spent time and effort in sorting out our
mess without charging one penny. Although it was going to be
an up-hill struggle he had worked out a way we could manage
to make all the repayments necessary, but at the same time
enable us to meet the other demands on our finances. This
having been sorted out was a great strain off our shoulders.

One of the things which did help was Sue next door insisting
I go with her for a food parcel each week. The food parcel group
had sufficient funds to enable them to carry on their good work
for five or six weeks after the return to work. These helped
many, many families back on to the treadmill of ordinary life
and to ease the hardships they had to face on the long road to
recovery from their own financial quagmire.

Life did settle down again, but this time our roles reverted
back to Don going out to work, while I stayed at home. Learning
to be 'just a housewife' again. I found this very hard. And my
health didn't improve much. One reason was the eternal wait

for Don's trial to be heard in the Crown Court, Sheffield. The second reason was due to the fact that I felt guilty — guilty because I wasn't helping Don pay the debts off.

I felt that I should have somehow shrugged off my illness by perhaps taking a short sick leave, then, when I felt better, returning to work. But I also had a great sense of guilt having let Don down, when he had needed my support more than any other time in our marriage and during his suspension.

Instead of helping him, what had I done? Gone to pieces!

Would he ever trust me again, should a future crisis happen? The 'if onlys' went around and around inside my head. In the end I became listless and didn't have much interest in anything, including my own family.

I couldn't read or do anything that I would normally do when I wanted to relax. Even television couldn't hold my attention for long. Because instead of 'watching' a programme, I would be wondering how they had filmed that particular bit, or where the camera man must have been to have taken that shot, or it was a case of 'I saw Ian (Look North's camera man) do something like that'. So I thought television a complete waste of time.

A few weeks after Don's return to work, after the children were bedded down for the night, Don came into the room where I had been sitting staring at the screen but as usual not even aware of the programme. He turned the set off and sat down beside me.

'Right Mrs Keating, you're going to tell me just what is bugging you. Is it something I've done? If you would only talk about it, I might be able to help. You're obviously not working it out yourself, are you?'

I told him there was nothing wrong and would he please switch the television back on, because I was interested in the programme. Don said he would sit there all night if he had to, because he was going to get to the bottom of it.

After a while I started to tell him just how I felt. He interrupted initially to say I was the most muddle-headed woman he had ever met. He had guessed right, about my guilty feelings about not earning money to help him, but the other guilt, he would never have guessed about in a hundred years. Although, having known me so long, he said, he should have realised really.

He went on to say that what I hadn't remembered during my guilt trip, was that I had been there many other times. I had stayed with him all the way through the strike and, for him, the most important time was being able to see me waiting for him outside the courthouse.

Like other married couples, having gone through the hard and bad times together, we realised that night, that we had shared many things but not our innermost feelings with all that that entailed. That night we talked, exchanging all the pain, hurt and anguish we had both felt throughout the strike. Sometime in the early hours we went to bed. During those hours, we came to a renewed understanding between us. We still share that to the present day.

CHAPTER FIFTEEN

Innocence
'All the charges have been dropped'

In August 1985, one year and two months after his arrest, Don and I walked into the Crown Court at Sheffield. We were both filled with trepidation about how the court case would go. Although we had been heartened by the fact that some of the men arrested on the same day as Don, who had been brought to trial first on riot charges, had, on the forty-second day, had their trial stopped by the judge. The case was thrown out of court, the charges were struck off the records and the costs should then be paid out of public funds. To fully understand about this trial you would really have to read a book already published about Orgreave and the subsequent court case, called *The Battle For Orgreave*, written by one of the arrested men, Bernard Jackson.

During the first couple of hours everyone sat around in the waiting room, making conversation, reading the papers, lying around and drinking endless cups of tea or coffee. Gareth Pearce made an appearance a short while later, to say that the barrister representing the prosecution would be willing to stop the trial if all the men would be willing to accept a bind-over — which, to the men, was in effect, like an admission of guilt. So it was refused quite vehemently and out of hand.

Just before the lunch recess, at twelve noon, the men were called together again and the bind-over was offered to them once more, but this time the prosecution would be willing to have the charges struck off the record.

Don was angry and at the same time adamant that we, as a family, hadn't suffered the anguish and worry of having these serious charges hanging over our heads for fourteen months, only to admit, on eventually coming to trial, that he had been guilty, when in fact he wasn't.

With this news being passed back to the prosecution, the waiting men were told that there was a recess for lunch and would we all be back for 1.45 pm.

Don and I were among the early ones back in the waiting room, where we watched the room filling up once again, as the people returned in small groups, from wherever they had lunched.

Quietly at first, a murmur then a rumour began to circulate the room, that the prosecution had decided to drop all charges. Don, being Don, wouldn't believe a word of it, he wasn't going to get his hopes up on speculation. While everyone else was kissing and giving bear hugs to each other, Don and I stood there together, waiting and praying this was all true.

It wasn't until Mike Mansfield, the barrister acting on behalf of Don and the other men, appeared from a room to confirm that the charges were now dropped and Don was acquitted, that we realised it was over, finally it was over.

We looked at each other scarcely believing our own ears, we were relieved, bewildered, happy and yet still sad. Now, Don would never be able to say in public just what had happened. Never would he be able to tell the wider public that he had been innocent from the word go.

It was wonderful to return home, to collect our children from my parents who had been taking care of them. To go home knowing that the huge burden had finally been lifted from our shoulders.

Sometime the next day, television brought Chief Constable Wright to the screen to say that the whole matter would be dropped now. The police had in effect had the charges dropped to help bring a reconciliation between them and the miners, and he hoped that the leniency would help to bring this about.

Since then this has been one of the hardest things to bear, to know that the country at large would never know that the men had been acquitted purely and simply because they were innocent, and the defence had so much evidence to prove just that, that the prosecution couldn't in fact carry on.

I suppose the real truth of it was, it wouldn't have done for the whole truth to emerge in its entirety and 'the powers that be' made quite sure that the public didn't find out the real truth, which was a far cry from the one portrayed on television that fateful day.

CHAPTER SIXTEEN

Finally
'No one will read it'

Despite everything, our decision to strike, to fight for his job, was the right one; without a job our future would have been very bleak indeed. All the hardships and heartache have been more than worth a year's sacrifice for a secure future. All we ever wanted was a job and the self-respect that it brings.

I won't let a day go by without hoping that the whole truth with many aspects of the strike will one day be revealed to the whole country. Maybe one day some journalist or MP will uncover enough evidence to bring this about.

Count the cost! It may be a cliche, but Cortonwood Colliery had been the heart of the community, providing jobs and security; it had shaped the village and brutalised the landscape. Now we were having to live without it.

A few months after the closure in 1986 I returned to visit what remained of the colliery. No one would have believed a pit had been there: what had been a jumble of squat buildings, dominated by the headgear and the spinning wheels, was a black plain, pockmarked and littered with rubble and debris. My walk had started when it was warm and sunny but by the time I had reached the end of the broken tarmac lane it had turned chilly, adding to the feeling of a windswept plain. No familiar buzz of human activity, no rhythmic humming or throbbing of machinery, just an almost audible silence and the spoil heaps in the distance. It looked as if someone, somewhere high in the British Coal management structure, had decided that the pit had to be flattened in one blow. Other mines had closed but their empty surface buildings had remained intact for months, in some cases for years. From the air the closed pits, from Darton to Doncaster, must have looked like so many rotting hulks. Cortonwood, which had been the symbol of NUM resistance during the strike, a familiar sight on television, did not survive long enough to be one of the hulks.

Cortonwood and the strike were indelibly linked in the public eye. So the pit — and consequently memories of the strike — had to be wiped out immediately. The 'Alamo', the pickets' hut at the end of the pit lane, which the NUM branch had wanted to preserve on another site, was the first building to be bulldozed. The rest soon followed.

I looked round to see if a plaque had been left in memory of the men who had worked there since its opening in the early 1870s. Many men had been maimed or killed over the years; even more had left to lose their lives in two world wars. There was nothing, perhaps another manifestation of the lack of warmth exhibited by the accountants who now run the industry. I turned to go back, filled with sadness. Surely the men at the pit had been worthy of a mention.

I still visit the site once or twice a year. On my last visit I noticed concrete pillars had been erected, like tombstones, on top of the shafts. A brass plaque in the centre of one of the pillars reads: *British Coal, South Yorkshire Area, No. 1 shaft, capped May 1988* (capped: a term used to describe the way a shaft is filled in to avoid the possibility of mining subsidence and the emission of underground methane gas). There was still no mention of the men. But at least half the winding wheel — part of the equipment used to wind men and coal to the surface — had been saved and placed outside the parish hall, a simple memorial to the pit's link with the village.

With the closure of the pit, many people believed Brampton would become a ghost village — but that did not happen.

Instead, the community was split into two camps. On the one hand the families who accepted what they believed to be lucrative redundancy payments from British Coal were smiling, full of well being. The money enabled them to go out and buy new clothes, cars, caravans, electrical goods or new furnishings for their homes. The burden of debt was lifted off their shoulders. On the other hand were the men who had turned down redundancy and who were transferred to other pits.

The latter were the ones who had difficulties at that time. At work relationships between men and management were appalling. The deputies (pit foremen), many of whom had been friends and neighbours, were ignored. The miners who kept their jobs did not have lump sums to pay off their debts. It took Don and me three years to repay everything we owed. The mortgage people allowed us two years to pay off one year's arrears. Electricity, telephone and rates bills put immense pressure on families, but eventually we got to the end of that tunnel. Then we had to replace all the things that had worn out over the previous four years.

Over a four- or five-year period the situation and the community with it turned turtle. The men who had accepted redundancy now found their world crumbling. Most of the men had envisaged a new life out of the pit but it soon became apparent that the very few jobs available were poorly paid and the working hours were long. Many men found their redundancy money, instead of being a nice nest egg, had dwindled away because there were no jobs. Others took no sound financial advice and invested on the stock market at a time when share prices were racing ahead at an abnormal rate, and therefore they lost their money in the crash of October 1987.

The closure of the pit heralded the withdrawal of British Coal from the village. Soon the former Coal Board houses were bought by the sitting tenants or by large property companies which converted them into bed-sits. Brampton, once a quiet community, saw the return of the police. This time they were not involved in clashes with pickets — but were called in to quell fights and domestic disturbances in the bed-sits. It wasn't long before the locals were sick and tired of what was happening and petitioned Rotherham Borough Council. So the council stopped issuing licences to landlords. The tenants, many of whom were youngsters who were becoming more and more unhappy about their living conditions, left the area. Peace and quiet returned to Brampton. Most of the bed-sits have now been sold to decent people to make decent homes.

The closure of the pit resulted in other changes in our lives. Don was transferred to another colliery in October 1985. There was apprehension as to how he and his mates would be accepted at the new pit, Barnburgh, a distance of four miles from our home. There had been a rumour the Barnburgh miners would give the former Cortonwood men problems because the Cortonwood men had voted to close Cortonwood. The trouble did not materialise; quite the opposite occurred — the Barnburgh men were fantastic, a tribute to every man at the pit. However, history was soon to repeat itself and Barnburgh Colliery was in trouble. In 1985 there had been assurances that Barnburgh had fifteen years of coal reserves; but that did not stop British Coal putting it into the review procedure, in other words its future was in jeopardy. It could not match the new economic yardsticks laid down by management.

Again, the men voted to close the pit. The men who wanted to leave the industry and accept the so-called generous redundancy payments outnumbered the miners who wanted to keep their jobs. Again, Don was on the move, this time to Maltby Colliery where he is still employed.

The post strike period found me rather restless and I suppose discontented with life. Change, at home and at work, was becoming the key word. Unimportant incidents rankled and I began to question my role in life. Didn't anyone see me as a person in my own right? It was at that time I began to question other things in life: my life-style, my relationship with my husband and children — even my own identity. To be a wife, a mother who helped out financially by taking low-paid jobs — was that to be my sole role in life? What was I capable of? What could I offer the outside world? So many questions, never any answers. I had no academic qualifications. My childhood and teenage years had been so conditioned that I actually believed that education was wasted on girls and that my future lay with marriage and children. The contradictory impulses in my mind were disturbing. After the strike I could not return to being a housewife. Where should I start? Without doubt back at the beginning, with my so-called education.

With help from the local library I started on the long road to self-fulfilment and I contacted an adult literacy centre in Barnsley. At first I found the prospect of admitting I had a problem quite daunting, but I now smile at the amount of time I spent pacing the pavement outside the centre in Eldon Street, Barnsley, trying to find the courage to walk through the front door. Eventually I grasped the nettle. Thirty minutes later I left Christine Midgley's office on quite a high. There hadn't been any embarrassment, and I think at that moment I stopped hating myself for being a failure.

I started work with my tutor, Sheila Morton, the following week. I didn't know what to write about. The blank piece of paper glared back. What do you write about eighteen years after leaving school? 'Write about the strike — you'll know about that,' she said, 'and don't worry about the content, no one will read it.' Two mornings a week were spent at the centre improving my standard of grammar and spelling; at home I plodded on with the essay on the strike. When I had nearly finished, Sheila dropped the bombshell: 'Would you consider having it published?' I was speechless. The rapport with her had enabled me to wash away my pain and frustration in the flow of words that were for her eyes only. No one but no one was ever going to read those words. After all, they contained too much hurt, too much of my hidden self. The thought of those police officers who had taunted me by waving the wads of pound notes from behind their van windows, when I was virtually penniless, rushed back. How they would gloat! They would castigate the book. Then there was the television director's cynical and sarcastic attitude. Oh, yes! Reading my book would give him immense pleasure. He had treated me like dirt beneath his feet.

With hindsight I realise my thoughts could be interpreted as being egotistical and probably unfair. So I can only apologise for my thoughts. The truth had to come out. If I wasn't prepared to do it, I could not expect others to tell the public what went off in the mining villages during the strike. Later my mood changed; I thought it had been a waste of time — who wanted to read a book written by a housewife?

Meanwhile, I had been considering attending college on a full-time basis. I broached the subject with Don who was stunned . . . I could not be serious. What about the children? Our home, our marriage? It wasn't possible to attend college full-time, study at home and still run a family and home. Residential college was even more out of the question. Had I taken leave of my senses! Reality reasserted itself. It was just a dream. I couldn't sleep. I had at my fingertips what a lot of people never experienced — a good stable marriage. Not only do I love my husband, I have two lovely children; what more could I want? I flitted from one bedroom to another, peering at the sleeping faces of the children. They hadn't asked to be born; it was our decision. We both had wanted the children who had given us so much pleasure. So why the hell was I putting all this at risk? What had happened? No, I couldn't and wouldn't go to college. It would lead to the collapse of the marriage. Just the thought brought me so much anguish. So I reached a compromise.

Maybe what I wanted was to go out and meet people. The naive young lady had gone, for it was now time to see what life was like outside the confines of our family home and the mining community. How could this be achieved? The answer came a few months later. By that time my essay had been typed up. I still didn't have a clue what to do with it, so I was quite happy to leave it in a drawer.

A little later I came across an envelope containing a letter and a book which I received in November 1985. A man called Brian Lewis had heard an interview by Richard Wells on the 'Today' radio programme featuring Don and me. Brian thought we had gone a long way towards explaining the reasons behind the miners' strike and he sent a book to our children. When I re-read the letter, I realised Brian had a hand in publishing. The logo on the first page of the letter read: *Everyone has a story to tell. Yorkshire Arts Circus finds ways of helping them to tell it.* When I contacted Brian, who had now moved to Castleford, he wanted to see the manuscript. Brian read the manuscript and much to my pleasure said it should be published. Unfortunately, he didn't see a market for it, mainly because books about the strike had swamped the market in recent months. Brian had published a couple of these books and didn't want to commit any more resources to that topic. What he could do, however, was have the manuscript made into book form.

Rather than pay them cash — which was still in short supply in our household — I decided to work for him as payment in return for having 20 copies printed. Brian and his workers went out into the community to research and interview the general public. The results were then put together in a series of short paragraphs to form a book. The first book, *Pit Pants, Every Four Pegs* was researched in the small town of South Elmsall.

Initially, I was very nervous about approaching and interviewing people. But that's what I wanted to do and I gritted my teeth. Some of the interviews were interesting, others mundane, all were revealing. One was both pathetic and amusing. When I asked one young man about his ambitions he leaned forward and whispered: 'Do you know what I really want to do?' The alarm bells rang but I couldn't resist asking: 'No, please tell me.' He replied: 'I want to make love to Princess Diana.' His contribution ended in the waste bin.

I worked on three books in other locations after that and did, thankfully, get my act together. I helped out with *Innings and Outings* based on Monk Bretton, *Privy to Privatisation* (South Kirkby and South Elmsall) and lastly, my favourite, *The Bus to Barnsley Market* which covered my locality, Wombwell and Darfield.

I still managed to come across the occasional, comical interview, including one concerning a middle-aged woman who worked as a home help. One day while cleaning the home of a widow who was well into her eighties she found a condom in the window-sill. Not really knowing how to broach the subject, or whether it was wise to do so, she hesitated and then took the plunge. Mrs W: 'Do you know what this is?' Old lady: 'Of course I do - it's a condom.' Mrs W: 'And do you know what it is used for?' Old lady: 'Of course I do, silly, it's for condomsation.'

My manuscript was printed in book form but my association with Yorkshire Arts Circus, sadly, featured less and less in my life. Don and I realised that we had to take stock of our financial situation. Determined to find a job, I acquired an application form from one firm only to be told I was too old. What a slap in the face, past your 'sell by date' at thirty-three!

In April 1987, I became an auxiliary night nurse at a private residential home, the duties of which I literally learnt on my feet. My duties involved putting the residents to bed, dealing with their personal needs at night, hourly checks, bed changes, and then try to wash and dress as many of them as I could before the shift ended at 7.30 am. The job was a mixture of good and bad: one problem involved dealing with sometimes aggressive patients suffering from senile dementia. Another problem concerned avoiding the amorous advances of elderly male patients, for the advancing years had not curbed their enthusiasm one little bit. Yet there was much pleasure in the job, for many of the senior citizens had lots of warmth and wisdom. I wish I had retained all the useful information I picked up from them.

There was also sadness and sorrow. One old lady shocked me when she said she felt she was on death row just waiting for death to claim her. With the disposal of her home and possessions, she had no escape route, only death. Her plight cut deep; I felt so inadequate.

In the post strike period I have also worked in a factory, done a stint as a community youth worker and made lampshades.

The strike left many indelible marks on the family. Two aspects, however, returned to haunt us in the aftermath. In the strike we had a love-hate relationship with the media. Before March 1984, our contact with newspapers, television and radio had been non-existent. In the midst of the dispute we found ourselves pitchforked into the limelight. Sometimes we were embarrassed when we saw and heard ourselves on television, angry when crucial scenes were edited out of the programme. On the other hand, I found some of the journalists and television crews interesting and stimulating. I was given new insights into the world of the media, not all bad. Don had always been suspicious of them but I gradually broke down his resistance.

But five years after the end of the strike an incident left us stunned and bewildered. We were asked to take part in a television interview. Don wasn't too keen, as he thought there was not much use going over old ground. The strike was history. Both of us, however, did our best to help. Half-way through the interview we realised we were being set-up. The interviewer switched topics and started telling us that while our family were struggling during the strike Arthur Scargill had a great deal of money at his disposal, money donated by Russian miners and the Libyan government. My mind was in turmoil as I tried to understand what was happening and yet still try to continue with the interview. Obviously this was going to be an anti Arthur Scargill interview and we didn't want any part of it.

After the departure of the television crew, the repercussions of the evening's events started to sink in — we felt powerless. The film had been shot on 28 February and was due to be screened in the Cook Report on 5 March 1990. Those few days seemed like a lifetime. What would appear on television? After Don's anger had subsided I promised I would never allow another journalist in the house. In Don's view they had accepted and abused our hospitality. When the programme was screened, and everyone else was trying to digest the allegations re 'missing' Russian and Libyan money, I was hoping that none of the material dealing with my parents and my family would be included. It was a relief when the credits started to roll . . . we had been spared more anguish.

The media created problems for us; so had the police. Like most other mining families who had never been in trouble, we had viewed the police through rose-coloured glasses before the strike. Our image of them had been formed by a constant stream of television programmes depicting policemen as rather glamorous and crusading men, rather cynical perhaps, but nevertheless men who were champions of the law. The strike changed all that. I'll never forget what I witnessed during the strike: the sight of police clubbing British miners did not seem to fit in with the British way of life, although I realise that not all miners were innocent.

Five years after the end of the strike we found ourselves dealing with the police again. It was the one thing that all parents dread. A motorist tried to pick up Nikki on her way to school. He pulled up beside her on the pretext of asking directions, then tried to drag her inside. Realising something was wrong the following morning — she was white and nervous — I finally got the story out of her. Trembling, she said she had not mentioned anything because she knew we would compel her to tell the police. Her fear of the police was equal, if not greater, than her fear of the abductor. It took me some time to calm her down long enough for her to allow me to contact the police. She really believed the police would not accept her version of the incident because there were no witnesses. It took Nikki a while to regain her confidence. Six weeks later he pulled in front of her again. This time she ran to her boyfriend's and called the police herself. At least her attitude towards the police was changing.

There was plenty of good news in 1990. Early in the year I received a letter from Wharncliffe Publishing in Barnsley — they had decided to publish the book. It had been a long haul from those early days when I stared at a blank piece of paper at the Adult Literacy Centre. Now a new chapter had opened in my life.

CHAPTER SEVENTEEN

The Last Years
1984-88 in Photographs

Above: Cortonwood Colliery at the beginning of the strike.

Above: The start of the Miners' Strike: March 1984. Yorkshire miners' President, Jack Taylor (right) and General Secretary, Owen Briscoe, announce that the miners' council have decided to call a strike over the closure of Cortonwood. My husband, Don, is third from the left at top of photograph.
Below: March 1984. Miners congregate outside NUM headquarters after rumours that the union's assets were to be seized.   Photos: John Marshall

Above: Women's Day of Action in Barnsley in May, 1984. The women played an important role during the miners' strike. Photo: John Marshall
Below: Miners and their wives in festive mood at a rally in Barnsley.

Both pages: Late 1984. Police, mounted and on foot, line-up for a night of confrontation with pickets in Knollbeck Lane, Brampton, near Cortonwood Colliery. The trouble started after a miner went back to work before the end of

the strike. The bowling green roller (top left) was pushed down Knollbeck Lane towards the police lines. (Below) A television camera team was on the spot of a fire at the house adjoining a shop in the Lane. Photos: Tony Simpson

Both pages: (Above and opposite page top) March 1985. The strike is over and miners return to work under one banner. Don is in the crowd. The Alamo, the pickets' hut (also pictured below at Christmas time) is on the left. It was demolished within a few days. (Bottom right) The remnants of Cortonwood pit, October 1986.

Above: The shafts at Cortonwood were capped in 1988. After the pit closure, the surface buildings and headgear were demolished in almost indecent haste, as if everyone wanted to eradicate the bitter memories of one of the biggest industrial disputes since 1926 as quickly as possible. All that remains: a road, spoil heaps and the concrete pillars.